LIFELONG

LEARNING

SKILLS

How to teach today's children for tomorrow's challenges

Jo-Anne Lake

Pembroke Publishers Limited

For Maurice, who best exemplifies lifelong learning

© 1997 Pembroke Publishers Limited
538 Hood Road
Markham, Ontario, Canada L3R 3K9

Canadian Cataloguing in Publication Data

Lake, Jo-Anne
  Lifelong learning skills: how to teach today's children for tomorrow's challenges

Includes bibliographical references and index.
ISBN 1-55138-089-7

1. Education, Elementary.   I. Title.

LB1555.L33 1997   372   C97-931432-1

Editor: Kate Revington
Design: John Zehethofer
Cover Photography: Ajay Photographics
Typesetting: Jay Tee Graphics Ltd.

Printed and bound in Canada
9 8 7 6 5 4 3 2 1

Contents

. . . .

CHAPTER ONE

A Vision of Lifelong Learning

The important thing is to keep moving ahead. Even if you're on the right track, you'll get run over if you just sit there.

Will Rogers, quoted in *Pathways to Performance*

The days of believing that learning is finished at graduation are over. Technology and global competition are transforming the workplace; a work role that was in demand last year may not exist next year. As Brian Stanfield wrote in the September 1996 issue of *Edges*, education is shifting from its school-bound, child-bound, time-bound focus to lifelong learning. In a world of accelerated metamorphosis, lifelong learning is the blueprint to embracing change ("Research Soundings: Plumblining the 90's").

A Shift in Educational Focus

Our new challenge is to prepare students to cope with a fast-changing world. In *Six Thinking Hats*, Edward de Bono writes: "Classrooms have been dominated by attempts to transmit knowledge or content. There is more to education than the attainment of knowledge." Our students will need to see education as a continuing process in their lives. They will need to know how to use many different learning methods, both old and new, and to develop transferable skills. They will need to have not only a foundation of knowledge acquired in school but also the ability to acquire new knowledge easily and skilfully. Soon it will be the norm for individuals to hone and broaden their skills constantly through reading, training courses, and intensive study. As Alvin Toffler wrote in *The Third Wave*, "The future is fluid — not frozen."

When I first read how the European Commission on Education and Training Programs defined lifelong learning, I felt daunted. The Commission defined lifelong learning as "the development of human potential through a continuously supportive process which stimulates and empowers individuals to acquire all the knowledge, values, skills and understanding they will require throughout their lifetimes and to apply them with confidence, creativity and enjoyment in all roles, circumstances and environments." Lifelong learning is embedded in my very soul: What meaningful and practical suggestions could I offer to educators to clarify their thoughts on the subject?

Just as I was about to leave this onerous task of clarifying what lifelong learning means, I reflected on Plutarch's line "the mind is not a vessel to be filled, it is a fire to be kindled." As well, I remembered what Benjamin Hoff says about scholars in *The Tao of Pooh*.

> *Owl:* But sometimes the knowledge of the scholar is a
> bit hard to understand because it doesn't seem to
> match up with our own experience of things. In other
> words, Knowledge and Experience do not necessarily
> speak the same language. But isn't the knowledge
> that comes from experience more valuable than the
> knowledge that doesn't? It seems fairly obvious to
> some of us that a lot of scholars need to go outside
> and sniff around — walk through the grass, talk to
> the animals. That sort of thing.
> *Pooh:* Lots of people talk to animals.
> *Owl:* Maybe, but . . . Not very many listen, though.
> *Pooh:* That's the problem.
> *Owl:* In other words, you might say that there is more
> to Knowing than just being correct.

Hoff's thoughts, as portrayed in the discussion above, uncovered yet another part of what it is to become a lifelong learner. When I revisited the Commission's statement "lifelong learning as a continuously supportive process," I was able to sketch out my vision of lifelong learning. You can see my Portrait of Lifelong Learning, which shows principles, personal traits that support lifelong learning, and essential transferable skills, on the facing page.

A Portrait of Lifelong Learning

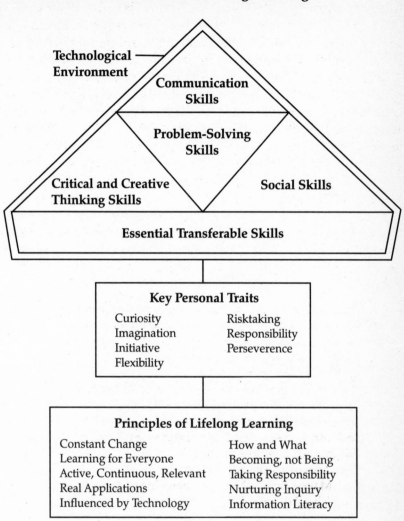

Internalizing the skills and concepts implicit in this Portrait of Lifelong Learning should help strengthen your commitment to promoting lifelong learning. Once you integrate many of its components within your classroom, you will gain some certainty that you are on the right track to enabling students to learn and grow as lifelong learners. This should inspire hope in you for the next generation for whom, more than ever, lifelong learning is essential.

Key Components of the Lifelong Learning Portrait

First of all, a lifelong learning culture is needed. The 10 principles I have identified are the building blocks to developing and sustaining such a culture. Recognizing these principles collectively, and acknowledging and understanding their significance, is essential in the development of a lifelong learning culture.

The traits identified as part of the Portrait suggest the personal qualities learners need in order to succeed in their lifelong learning quest. Underpinning many of them is the need for self-esteem. Nathaniel Branden, a psychologist and self-esteem specialist, writes: "Positive self-esteem is the cardinal requirement of a fulfilling life" (*How to Raise Your Self-Esteem*). Feelings of adequacy and self-acceptance are vital to learning new concepts and experiencing new activities. As teachers, we need to acquire a working knowledge of self-concept theory and to practise appropriate skills and strategies for enabling us to foster positive self-images in our students. Self-esteem expert Barbara Coloroso, in *Kids Are Worth It!*, shares six critical life messages for us to impart to them:

I believe in you.	You are listened to.
I trust in you.	You are cared for.
I know you can handle it.	You are very important to me.

It is also important that we see parents as partners to ensure that all students have the same opportunity to learn and grow. Fostering learning environments that provide for acceptance, love, concern, encouragement, sincerity, empathy, sensitivity, and understanding will provide opportunities for children to acquire the personal traits outlined in my Portrait.

The essential transferable skills are the foundation skills of lifelong learning. Since it is no longer possible to teach all available information, we must teach the skills needed to make the best use of information. Alvin Toffler, in *Learning for Tomorrow*, says: "The heart of the education program is not the information with which one becomes acquainted but the communication, information processing, problem solving and cognitive skills that are developed or acquired through understanding a body of knowledge." These skills are naturally interconnected, set within a technological environment. Robert K. Logan, author of *The Fifth Language*, reinforces Toffler's view of the skills required for lifelong learning.

We will need to create the right classroom learning environment: one where students can demonstrate how they think and reason clearly and critically, and access and evaluate information to solve problems. Our role is to help students to develop a portfolio of generic, transferable skills and strategies. The ultimate goal: For them to develop skills that are fully transferable throughout a lifetime.

Lifelong Learning Skills aims to spark and fan the flames of teachers fostering lifelong learning. It explores how teachers can promote in their classrooms essential transferable skills and the personal traits that underpin them. It outlines principles which, at work, foster a lifelong learning culture. It also strives to show how interrelated the dynamic components of my Portrait of Lifelong Learning are.

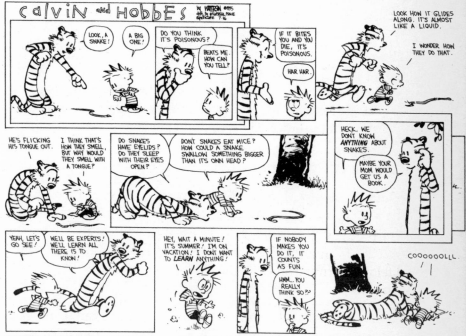

. . . .

CHAPTER TWO

The Principles of Lifelong Learning

I hear and I forget. I see and I remember. I do and I learn.

Ed Labinowicz, The Piaget Primer

The 10 principles noted in my Portrait of Lifelong Learning are fundamental to understanding the lifelong learning concept. They range from an appreciation of constant change to a recognition of the importance of information literacy.

Change Is Constant

In anthropologist Margaret Mead's words, "A person is born into one kind of world, grows up in another, and by the time his/her children are growing up, lives in still a different world." When my mother went to a one-room school in the Agricultural era, the main purpose of education was to provide a basic knowledge of reading, writing, and arithmetic. The community was a valued educational resource, with projects one big community partnership. The teacher, parents, and community, as a whole, worked together to provide real-life experiences that were relevant and purposeful for the students. The hands-on Gardening Project, outlined on page 11, helped my mother to develop essential transferable skills and practical gardening skills.

Alvin Toffler, in *The Third Wave*, notes that, like the Agricultural and Industrial eras before it, the Information Revolution is affecting the fabric, pace, and substance of our lives. Jim Clemmer, in

Education in the Agricultural Era

GARDENING PROJECT

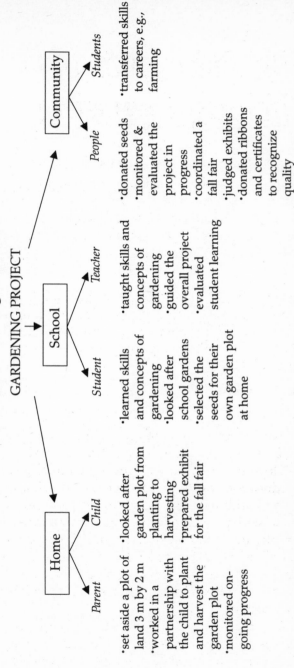

Home

Parent
- set aside a plot of land 3 m by 2 m
- worked in a partnership with the child to plant and harvest the garden plot
- monitored on-going progress

Child
- looked after garden plot from planting to harvesting
- prepared exhibit for the fall fair

School

Student
- learned skills and concepts of gardening
- looked after school gardens
- selected the seeds for their own garden plot at home

Teacher
- taught skills and concepts of gardening
- guided the overall project
- evaluated student learning

Community

People
- donated seeds
- monitored & evaluated the project in progress
- coordinated a fall fair
- judged exhibits
- donated ribbons and certificates to recognize quality achievement

Students
- transferred skills to careers, e.g., farming

11

Pathways to Performance, augments Toffler's view of the accelerated pace of change:

- Technological change has gone from evolutionary to revolutionary.
- Communication, seen not so long ago as delayed, multi-staged, and controlled, has become instant, direct, and uncontrollable.
- Innovation, formerly important, is now critical.
- Authority no longer derives from position, but from persuasion.

"Just as our success in the industrial age depended on a school system that taught us how to read and write, add and subtract, our success in the information age depends on a school system that teaches us how to manage information, utilize technologies, innovate and — above all — think," said Bank of Montreal chairman Matthew Barrett (*Globe & Mail*, November 30, 1996).

Signs of change include the development of partnerships between schools and businesses and the extension of learning into the workplace. The change that best represents the concept of lifelong learning is learning on one's own after schooling is done.

Learning Is for Everyone

Lifelong learning applies to everyone. For example, my grandson, Benjamin, a preschooler, constantly observes and inquires about things in his environment. Whether it's about a chickadee's song, a twirling maple key, or ants building their home, he asks questions spontaneously. Similarly, I've seen this sense of lifelong learning in my daughter. While on a teaching assignment in Singapore, she used her leisure time to travel to distant places, always writing and sharing new experiences. On one occasion, she sent us a postcard from Bali, saying, "Yes, they still use oxen to plough the rice fields!" I have also seen my mother struggle with technological change. She recently learned how to set an alarm system put in place in her house.

Lifelong learners have an intrinsic desire to understand, to find out about new things, to affirm their thoughts about the old, to remain current. Their common characteristics allow us to understand that lifelong learning applies to everyone.

Learning Is Active, Relevant, and Continuous

Active learning is rooted in the work of John Dewey who, in *Philosophy of Education*, says, "Learning can only occur through doing things." Learning involves playing, working, exploring, planning, initiating, and communicating.

As educators we are challenged to provide opportunities for students to make the connection between real life and what they learn in school. For example, when my Grade 5 students explored the concept of friction, their work included discovering what friction had to do with the functioning of tires on an automobile. From there they found other places where the concept of friction was at work. I encouraged students to relate the concept to either the changing world around them or to imagine how friction could be used to change the world. Resource books such as David Macaulay's *The Way Things Work* can provide a springboard for students to launch new thoughts and ideas.

Relevant curriculum will involve all students. Programs such as Chemcom, in which students investigate a fish kill to determine how it happened, how it might have been prevented, and how it can be cleaned up, are taking hold. As students acquire the necessary background information by exploring resources ranging from the Internet to journal articles, they have many opportunities to read and analyze materials — to strengthen their literacy skills. In "What's Ahead in Elementary Education," Gerald Bracey notes that the interdisciplinary method of instruction allows students to recognize the interconnections of subject material and consider how it relates to the world outside the classroom (*Elementary Curriculum*). Real-world experiences make learning more purposeful and meaningful.

Schools need to work with their communities — parents, associations, and businesses — to best prepare students to function in an ever-changing world. But doing so should not signify the decline of such subjects as history, the arts, and physical education: these remain vehicles for the development of essential transferable skills.

Continuous learning is inevitable. The latest predictions show that people can expect to have six careers in a lifetime. An Employability Skills Profile, such as the one that follows, suggests skills and experiences that are important in today's marketplace. Continuous learning will allow us to adapt and evolve as we go along.

Employability Skills Profile: The Critical Skills Required of the Canadian Workforce

Academic Skills	Personal Management Skills	Teamwork Skills
Those skills which provide the basic foundation to get, keep and progress on a job and to achieve the best results	The combination of skills, attitudes and behaviors required to get, keep and progress on a job and to achieve the best results	Those skills needed to work with others on a job and to achieve the best results
Canadian employers need a person who can: **Communicate** •Understand and speak the languages in which business is conducted •Listen to understand and learn •Read, comprehend and use written materials, including graphs, charts and displays •Write effectively in the languages in which business is conducted **Think** •Think critically and act logically to evaluate situations, solve problems and make decisions •Understand and solve problems involving mathematics and use the results •Use technology, instruments, tools and information systems effectively •Access and apply specialized knowledge from various fields (e.g., skilled trades, technology, physical sciences, arts and social sciences) **Learn** •Continue to learn for life	Canadian employers need a person who can demonstrate: **Positive Attitudes and Behaviors** •Self-esteem and confidence •Honesty, integrity and personal ethics •A positive attitude toward learning, growth and personal health •Initiative, energy and persistence to get the job done **Responsibility** •The ability to set goals and priorities in work and personal life •The ability to plan and manage time, money and other resources to achieve goals •Accountability for actions taken **Adaptability** •A positive attitude toward change •Recognition and respect for people's diversity and individual differences •The ability to identify and suggest new ideas to get the job done — creativity	Canadian employers need a person who can: **Work with Others** •Understand and contribute to the organization's goals •Understand and work within the culture of the group •Plan and make decisions with others and support the outcomes •Respect the thoughts and opinions of others in the group •Exercise "give and take" to achieve group results •Seek a team approach as appropriate •Lead when appropriate, mobilizing the group for high performance

Source: Employability Skills Profile: What Are Employers Looking For? Brochure 1992 E/F (Ottawa: The Conference Board of Canada, 1992).

14

Applications Are Real

Learning to apply concepts, skills, and knowledge is a significant part of lifelong learning, and opportunities to do so are all around us. As educators we need to help our students find these opportunities, possibly forming partnerships with community and business organizations. Community service can be encouraged. And working with corporations such as Shell Canada, Canada Trust, and Consumers Gas can help fund projects.

Technology Influences Learning

We must seek to ensure that the most current technology is used: computer simulation, computer-assisted instructions, CD-ROM technology, and more. The critical question is, How do you make the most of technology in the classroom? In one instance, high school teacher Barbara Orr describes how students connect electronically with poets and novelists across Canada who act as mentors to the young writers, providing them with real-world connections to books and authors (*Globe & Mail* Technology Edition, August 15, 1996).

Integrating technology into a unit of study is worth pursuing and is becoming more common. For example, science teachers in Singapore have been learning to use computerized data banks, extract materials from various electronic sources, and create multimedia lessons. They will save time in preparing lessons and be able to choose between multimedia lessons from scratch or from predesigned packages. This whole new way of teaching will see teachers and students interacting via computer ("Opening Up New Vistas in Class Through Teaching by Computer," *International News*).

School libraries will evolve from library resource centres that provide learning materials and instruction to information centres that provide and coordinate the sharing of information of all kinds. From self-contained, collection-based facilities, they will become access-based services, part of global and interconnected information networks.

As educators we must encourage schools to develop an exciting, media-rich environment. If our schools are not yet on the Internet, then we should lobby for that. We should also explore integrating CD-ROM, video, and Internet projects. Staying abreast of new technological advancements will mean taking responsibility for our own learning.

The Learning Focus Is More on the How Than the What

Teaching students how to think will have a positive impact on their future as lifelong learners. In "Schools, Schooling & Teachers: A Curriculum for the Future," Thomas and Maureen Sheeran define schooling as both the process by which students are taught and the product that results from such teaching. The content constitutes the product and the method used to deliver the content constitutes the process (May 1996 *Bulletin*). Other researchers also believe that what we know cannot be separated from how we know.

Maintaining a balance between the how and the what will challenge educators. Learners will need to use a concept, as well as describe it. For example, Grade 5 students studying motion manipulated hands-on materials in small groups to discover what concepts such as gravity meant. They then demonstrated their understanding by putting together a phrase. After studying friction and inertia one group noted: "When friction strikes inertia stops."

Teaching information skills is now more important than imparting facts which may be obsolete tomorrow. This means providing students with the necessary tools to continue learning on their own.

Lifelong Learners Are Always in the Process of Becoming

In *The Velveteen Rabbit*, Margery Williams writes:

> "What is REAL?" asked the Rabbit one day. "Does it mean having things that buzz inside you and a stick-out handle?"
> "Real is not how you are made," said the Skin Horse. "It's a thing that happens to you. When a child loves you for a long, long time, not just to play with, but REALLY loves you, then you become Real. It doesn't happen all at once. You become. It takes a long time."

Just as the Rabbit spent a lifetime to become real, so too the learner strives throughout a lifetime to become a lifelong learner.

Learners Take Responsibility for Their Learning

In the past, the sole responsibility for learning rested on the teacher; now we *all* have to assume responsibility for our own learning. An Ohio University study confirmed the value of students venturing beyond traditional print resources. It found that the use of electronic communication contributed to student learning in courses ranging from math and music to management. In "Lecturers' reliance on Web assailed," journalist Mary Gooderham quotes Dr. Carl Cuneo: "The technology when used properly can be an invaluable time-saver and give students control over when and where they do their work" (*Globe & Mail*, January 7, 1997).

Inquiry Is Nurtured

We need to acknowledge and nurture the inquiring mind. "By inquiry we come to perceive the truth," observed French philosopher Pierre Abélard. In the classroom setting inquiry may occur spontaneously or may be taught. The method requires students to learn not only how to ask questions but how to collect data and how to form generalizations. Different topics lead to varying styles of inquiry — experimenting, interviewing, using library resources, exploring through drama or discussion, observing natural phenomena, using primary sources of information, and engaging in personal writing. As Judy Caulfield and Franca Fedele note in "Creating a Community of Learners," there is no formula for inquiry learning (*Inquiry Learning*, September/October 1996).

The discovery method is one common way to teach inquiry. For example, when I put my collection of spinning tops from around the world in my school's front display case, it sparked months of questions and students began their own collections and investigations. As Neil Postman suggests in *Teaching as a Conserving Activity*, we must do what we can to ensure that students don't leave school as periods rather than as question marks.

Students Demonstrate Information Literacy

Students need to be information literate to survive in tomorrow's world.

They need to know how to access, evaluate, and use the information they require regardless of the flood around them. The graphic "Information Literacy and Lifelong Learning" shows how information literacy interconnects in a lifelong learning environment. It shows critical and creative thinking, problem solving, and decision making circling the information centre, projecting the importance of skills in all forms of literacy. It identifies the three forms of information literacy: traditional literacy (the ability to read and write); media literacy (the ability to critically evaluate and create media, such as television, advertising, and news stories); and numerical literacy (the ability to understand and solve problems with data and numbers). A larger circle indicates the various ways in which we process information, that is, the way we acquire, critically evaluate, select, use, create, and communicate. Next, the graphic indicates the new information sources: these include on-line databases, the Internet, electronic bulletin boards, multimedia learning programs, CD-ROMs, and laserdisks. Finally, it raises the challenge of finding new ways to manipulate, analyze, communicate, and store information.

A Lifelong Learning Culture

By understanding and implementing the 10 principles of lifelong learning outlined in this chapter, we can influence what should be happening in our schools and workplace environments. Below is a summary of the principles which, at work, mark a lifelong learning culture.

The Nature of a Lifelong Learning Culture

Change is constant.
Learning is for everyone.
Learning is active, relevant, and continuous.
Applications are real.
Technology influences learning.
The learning focus is on the how more than the what.
Lifelong learners are always in the process of becoming.
Learners take responsibility for their learning.
Inquiry is nurtured.
Students demonstrate information literacy.

Information Literacy and Lifelong Learning

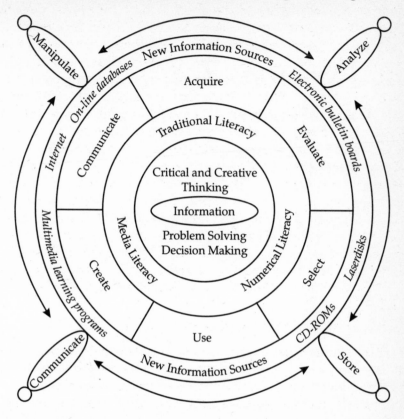

(Adapted from *Information Literacy and Equitable Access: A Framework for Change*, an Ontario Ministry of Education draft document)

A May 1993 ERIC Digest *article, Vicki Hancock's "Information Literacy for Lifelong Learning," defines information literacy as follows: an individual's ability to recognize a need for information, identify and locate appropriate information sources, know how to gain access to the information contained in those sources, evaluate the quality of information obtained, organize the information, and use the information effectively.*

....

CHAPTER THREE

Personal Traits That Support Lifelong Learning

What lies behind us and what lies before us are tiny
matters compared to what lies within us.

Ralph Waldo Emerson

The 21st century requires a different kind of person — one who
thinks, questions, innovates, and takes entrepreneurial risk —
write Alvin and Heidi Toffler (*Creating a New Civilization*). Although such individuals have always existed, they have been the
exception, not the norm. That must change, however. An overload
of information makes a school focus on content, on memorization
of facts, less valuable. We need to acknowledge and nurture
thinking, risktaking individuals, which is what most children
entering school are. Understanding how well the traits noted in
my Portrait of Lifelong Learning support lifelong learning is key
to their development.

A New Kind of Person

Although other traits support lifelong learning too, my Portrait
identifies these seven: curiosity, imagination, initiative, flexibility,
risktaking, responsibility, and perseverance. You may want to
visualize them as atoms which, when combined, create a pattern
of energy. Although the demand for these traits varies, depending
upon the situation and other circumstances beyond our control,

their presence or lack in a learner, as well as whether the learner draws upon them, will determine the extent to which the lifelong learning concept is embraced.

Personal Traits That Support Lifelong Learning

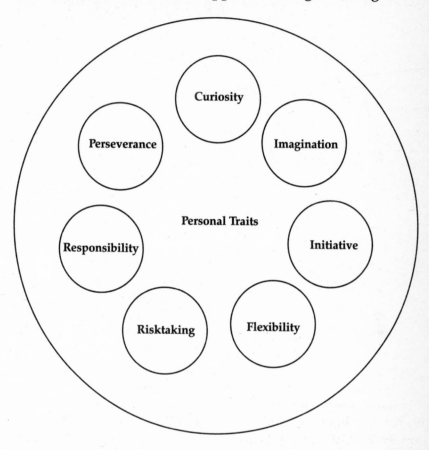

Each person brings to the learning environment personal traits that are subject to change and growth. In the home and at the school the learning environment nurtures and develops these traits through many learning opportunities, grounded in self-esteem.

In this chapter I will note each personal trait, suggest strategies for its development, recommend appropriate resources, and point out briefly how each trait influences a lifelong learning culture.

Curiosity

In his *Horn Book Magazine* article, "Dr. Seuss and Dr. Einstein: Children's Books & Scientific Imagination," Chet Raymo quotes Einstein as saying: "Mystery invites curiosity. Unless we perceive the world as mysterious we shall never be curious about what makes the world tick."

Mystery has been a driving force since the beginning of time. What is the black hole? What makes night and day? Who made the stars? Human beings, such as Alexander Graham Bell and Albert Einstein, have been curious and have kept trying to figure things out.

Children try to figure things out too. They ask themselves "Why?" "How?" and "What might happen if . . .?" over and over again. The number of times the question is repeated matters not. The goal, to search for the truth, is ever present. On a walk to a park, for example, my three-year-old grandson, Benjamin, asked, "How do you get down the storm sewer, Grandpa?" "Using a ladder," responded his grandpa. "But what other ways can you get down there?" inquired Benjamin. I have observed this sense of curiosity about the world in my students too.

To be curious is a natural inclination from birth to death. We can encourage curiosity by asking learners to inquire about what they perceive, read, and hear. We must capture children's interest early and find ways to nourish their natural enthusiasm and wonderment.

Promoting curiosity through children's literature

Most of the books featured in this resource are picture books which work well as teaching tools to help students develop whatever traits, skills, or strategies are necessary. I have successfully used stories with my students not only to promote a desirable personal trait but to introduce a theme, clarify a concept, introduce and strengthen appropriate skills, provide closure to a topic and, in general, reinforce learning. Initially I read the story orally to the whole class. For example, I once read Claude Clement's *The Voice of the Wood* to introduce a unit on Sound in my classroom. For follow-up I encouraged the students to bring from home any instruments they could to develop a learning centre for the Sound unit. As Marlene Asselin and others observe in *Storyworlds*, learning centres provide the vehicle for responding to stories and a means of constructing knowledge. They call for the exercise of imagination, social interactions, and language and thinking processes.

Using children's literature is a powerful way of instilling curiosity. Phil Cox's *Whatever Happened to Professor Potts?* invites Junior and Intermediate students to follow the trail of clues in search of the missing professor. Throughout the book there are codes to be cracked, clues to be spotted, and questions to be answered. *The 13th Clue*, by Ann Jonas, draws children of all ages into working out mysterious directions.

Books such as Margie Golick's curiosity-sustaining *Wacky Word Games* contain fascinating word games and picture clues. Students are drawn into the pages through the use of direct questions. "How many words can you think of that rhyme with 'thin'?" "Can you figure out how to turn lead into gold?"

Probing with a twist

Teaching should excite students' natural curiosity. For example, if you want someone to reflect, ask what questions the learner has asked. When I do this with my grandson, Ben, who is in nursery school, I enjoy waiting for a response because I know he is reflecting upon the day and thinking a little harder before he responds.

A teacher's questions should promote students' activity and reasoning. Reasoning questions are meant to make children think and reason independently about their own experiences, reflect upon the relationships they have discovered or recognized, and open up discussion. Questions that begin with "Have you seen" or "Do you notice" stimulate exploration and experimentation. "What happens if" questions probe for more than one-word answers and stimulate productive activity. In *Primary Science*, Wynne Harlen offers a useful set of guidelines for strengthening skills in asking productive questions. These are summarized below.

- Study the effect on children of asking different kinds of questions so that you can distinguish the productive from the unproductive.
- Use the simplest form of productive question: Have you seen . . .? Do you notice . . .?
- Use measuring and counting questions where appropriate: How often . . .? How long . . .?

- Use comparison questions: How are your structures alike and how do they differ?
- Use action questions to investigate relationships: What happens if you throw a tiny piece of paper into a spider's web?
- Use problem-posing questions: Can you find a way to . . .?

Making scientific inquiries

Scientific inquiry encourages individuality in children's approaches to problem solving. Children are provided with opportunities for discovery through following the process of exploring, questioning, predicting, observing, and explaining. For example, they might be challenged to build the tallest, strongest building possible using toothpicks and chickpeas that have been soaked overnight. After allowing students to explore materials ranging from straws to paper rolls, you could arrange them into groups of four. Be sure to let them ask questions, predict possibilities, and plan and collect materials for their project. Encourage group decision making in relation to the task and provide plenty of time for students to communicate and to evaluate the final structures, using criteria they help to develop. As far back as 1860, philosopher Herbert Spencer said: "Children should be led to make their own investigations and to draw their own inferences. They should be told as little as possible and induced to discover as much as possible."

Stephen Kramer's *How to Think Like a Scientist* and Sandra Markle's *Science Mini-Mysteries* are two valuable resources.

The influence of curiosity on lifelong learning

Margaret Boyce, in a *Toronto Star* Opinion piece, "Sense of Wonder Is Vital for Teachers of Any Faith," reminds us that wonder is a vital component of learning (February 24, 1996). Curiosity sparks inventions such as the television, the snowmobile, and the computer. It is the heartbeat of finding out things and applying the learning to create new things.

Imagination

A common understanding about imagination is evolving. We know that the way we imagine the future can have a powerful impact on the decisions we make today. In *The Seven Habits of Highly Effective People*, Stephen Covey notes that "imagination is an important tool for setting powerful goals."

Human imagination is the main source of value in the innovation economy, writes Don Tapscott (*The Digital Economy*). We know this to be true when we read classified ads to recruit imaginative individuals. "Realize what others can't even imagine. . . ." Gareth Morgan looks at creative ways of organizing and managing organizations through a way of thinking which he calls, in his book of the same title, imaginization. Businesspeople all attest to the importance of developing the imagination, and schools are trying harder to find strategies to tap students' imaginations, the heart of their mental energies. Through our imaginations, we create the future.

Promoting imagination through children's literature

Storybooks allow children to stretch their imaginations. In Elisa Schneider's *The Merry-Go-Round Dog*, a little girl finds the wooden tail of the old merry-go-round dog. From it she creates a special new playmate to warm the long wait for spring; she is then joyously reunited with an old merry-go-round friend. Liz Rosenberg creates a fantasy of courage and adventure in *The Carousel*. Two sisters find that the horses of a broken carousel have come alive in the rain. In *Andrew's Bath*, by David McPhail, Andrew imagines that many animals, including lions and elephants, accompany him in the tub. In this way he overcomes his fear of taking a bath alone.

Circus, by Peggy Roalf, consists of a series of books designed to present different painters' views of a single theme. Roalf stresses the use of imagination to approach the world as an artist would. She takes care to show a diversity in styles and techniques and suggests what we might look for in a painting. *Circus* helps learners explore the land where art and imagination meet.

Exploring what if

Using What If games is a powerful strategy to ignite the imagination. For example, "What would happen if you found your teddy bear could talk?" Such creative games may involve creating stories, ideas, pictures, and posters.

Stirring imagination through objects

Arrange for a curiosity corner in the classroom. Introduce unfamiliar objects that will challenge and stimulate children's imaginations: for example, toys from around the world. Display questions and invite students to ask their own questions. You could extend this idea by having students design and develop their own toys.

The influence of imagination on lifelong learning

Only imagination can create. Learning to nurture and value imagination will enhance our ability to effectively design and develop new creations in keeping with the rapid pace of technological development.

Initiative

When I think of initiative, words such as ambition, drive, self-motivation, energy, enthusiasm, and leadership come to mind. Many people in the world exhibit this energy, one being Donovan Bailey, Olympic and world champion in the 100 metre run: "My goal is to succeed at whatever I do. I've done that in athletics and I'll try to better myself, but when I leave track and field and go into the corporate world, I'll try to achieve the same status."

Belief in oneself, such as Bailey exemplifies, is a mindset that encourages one not only to spark the beginning of something but to stay the course and reach for the top. Research has shown that this attitude is developed during the early years, reinforced throughout childhood, and supported into our adult years. Bestowing encouragement fosters its development.

Promoting initiative through children's literature

Picture books provide models of desirable behavior. In Watty Piper's *The Little Engine That Could*, the little engine seizes the initiative and relies on determination — I think I can — to reach the goal. In *Willy the Wimp*, Anthony Browne encourages children to take the initiative to solve their own problems. A young chimpanzee, tired of being bullied by a suburban gorilla gang, decides to build up his muscles so he won't be a wimp anymore. In *Gobley for Mayor!*, Judi Gamble and Robert McConnell show how demonstrating initiative can reap dividends. Their story about a snail also shows how being flexible in thought and idea can have long-term benefits.

Establishing think bowls

Encourage students to work in small groups called Think Bowls. They should use their creative thinking skills to come up with unique ideas to solve specific problems. Be sure to expose students to a variety of situations that call for creative thinking. Encourage the transfer and extension of their ideas into practical use.

Developing board games

Allow time for students to design and develop a new game board. Extend their thinking by challenging them to plan and initiate a marketing campaign to get their product on store shelves.

The influence of initiative on lifelong learning

In "Job Skills Essential for Success, So Is Initiative," *Toronto Star* columnist Janis Kirk describes how initiative can contribute much to success (September 7, 1996). Considering the number of career changes they are expected to make, and the high rate of unemployment, students will need to take the initiative to learn and develop new skills throughout their lives.

Flexibility

The number of career changes students can look forward to points to the speed at which they will have to adapt. For this reason alone, we must prepare students to change their thinking quickly and react to new demands, such as retraining, as they arise. Those best prepared to absorb new ideas and to act upon them stand a better chance of adapting to the changes ahead.

Educators require flexibility too. We must be prepared to embrace changes in instructional methods, tools, and approaches in our campaign to open up opportunities for our students. Educational reform initiatives may have an impact on school year length,

educational delivery, accountability, and the use of business partnerships and information technology.

Promoting flexibility through children's literature

Children's literature can encourage flexibility. In *Something from
Nothing*, Phoebe Gilman demonstrates the benefits of being adapt-
able. An ingenious grandfather makes many things from his
grandson's favorite blanket as the grandson outgrows each piece
of clothing. *Abel's Island*, by William Steig, also provides many
examples of flexibility. A mouse stranded on an island must figure
out another way to return home after his first boat construction
fails.

Brainstorming

Brainstorming encourages flexibility of ideas. Provide many opportunities for students to generate ideas around a topic, concept,
issue, or concern. Refer often to Pembroke's *Brainstorm!*, by
Wendy Ashton Shimkofsky, and Margie Golick's *Wacky Word
Games*.

Creating working models

Provide a working model of a land vehicle to each small group of
students. Ask each group to devise a plan to alter their model in
such a way that it will function in water and/or in the air. Follow
up with a demonstration of all the models.

The influence of flexibility on lifelong learning

Flexibility is essential. In *The Digital Economy*, Don Tapscott writes,
"In the new economy you can expect to have to reinvent your
knowledge base throughout your life." If, for example, you've just
developed a great product, your goal is to produce a better one
that will make the first obsolete. Tapscott uses the example of
Microsoft making its own DOS, the best-selling software, obsolete
with the introduction of Windows 95.

Risktaking

To take risks is to have the willingness to be different, unusual. Great scientists such as Marie Curie, Alexander Graham Bell, and Albert Einstein have this characteristic. So do creative individuals such as Ludwig van Beethoven, T. S. Eliot, and Walt Disney. Risktaking has led to many accomplishments which have benefited humankind. Robert Frost's famous words "Two roads crossed paths, I took the road less travelled," taken from his poem "The Road Not Taken," remains an inspiration and source of comfort for others thinking about taking risks.

Promoting risktaking through children's literature

The Tunnel, by Anthony Browne, is an excellent story reinforcing the idea that risktaking can be beneficial. When a brother and sister discover a tunnel, the brother enters the tunnel freely while the sister stays timidly behind. When the brother does not return, the sister risks entering the tunnel in search of him.

David Weisner's *June 29, 1999* relates how a Grade 3 student, Holly, tackles an innovative science project. While her classmates are sprouting seeds in paper cups, Holly risks taking a different approach in her experiment. The success of her experiment encourages others to risk being different. This book also promotes imagination.

Brainstorming without fear

Brainstorming is the most effective method for generating creative ideas in the classroom. This technique works best when used in a risk-free environment where everyone observes guidelines for brainstorming, as clearly presented in Shimkofsky's *Brainstorm!*. Key pointers include the following: accept all ideas; say no to judging one another's ideas; refuse to discuss why ideas won't work; piggyback one idea on another. Be sure to provide many opportunities for students to brainstorm.

Preparing to go public

Speaking to an audience can be very risky, but you can show students how the key to successful public speaking is preparation.

Preparation means more than considering the kind of audience and the time frame. It encompasses making an outline to develop the topic, organizing the information in the order the speaker wishes to present it, practising diligently, and remembering to vary pitch, enunciate words, smile, and stand upright. *Speak Up! Speak Out!*, by Bob and Barbara Greenwood, helps students recognize the times when they need to organize their thoughts before they open their mouths. It offers 10 steps that make public speaking a snap, including how to zoom in on the topic; where to do research; when to rehearse; and why speakers should warm up. Familiarize students with the tips and techniques for feeling comfortable in any speaking situation. Provide opportunities for students to prepare and present topics of interest to small groups.

The influence of risktaking on lifelong learning

Whether it's the "Horse and Buggy" era or this era of rapid technological advancement, risktakers have led the way in lifelong learning, bringing us into the future.

Responsibility

From the time they are born until they enter school, children take on responsibility for their own learning. They willingly observe and explore their environment, asking questions to understand more about the world in which they live. Then they enter their years of formal schooling. Here responsibility for learning can slowly erode over the years.

The key to how we might encourage students to take responsibility for their own learning lies within Alvin Toffler's message that "all too often we are stuffing the heads of the young with the products of earlier innovation rather than teaching them how to innovate" (*Learning for Tomorrow*). In a climate of rapid technological change, the bottom line is that each of us will have to take responsibility to know what we need to know to function in our daily lives.

Promoting responsibility through children's literature

Sheila MacGill-Callahan follows the devastating environmental changes that have taken place over time throughout *And Still the Turtle Watched*. The message is simple: Care of the environment is everyone's responsibility. This story could serve as a springboard into discussion on other pressing environmental issues.

In Demi's *The Empty Pot*, Ping admits he is the only child in China unable to grow a flower from seeds distributed by the Emperor. The Emperor rewards Ping for his honesty. The author opens up possibilities for discussions on the responsibility of everyone to uphold honesty and other common societal values.

The Day That Henry Cleaned His Room, by Sarah Wilson, is a fun-loving story that can easily generate discussion about responsibility. Henry attracts the attention of reporters, scientists, and the army when he decides to clean up his room.

Providing opportunities for research on the Internet

Let students choose their own topic of interest for an independent project. Encourage them to focus on using the Internet for their data collection, while bearing in mind that its reliability may be in question. Advise students to consider the source of any information: What is the Web site? Is the document published? Is there a consistency between the Web site's theme and the qualifications of the person providing information? Work collaboratively with the students to develop timelines and set criteria for evaluation.

Fostering cooperative learning

Provide many opportunities for students to work in cooperative group settings (see Chapter 7). Also, allow them to make group decisions, for example, evaluating each other's performance and the group's overall performance.

The influence of responsibility on lifelong learning

Change is happening all around us at an unimaginable rate of speed. Unless we accept responsibility for our own learning, we cannot enter the lifelong learning culture.

Perseverance

What sets a successful person apart is not so much knowledge or strength but the will to succeed. The words determination, steadfastness, and internal motivation come to mind when thinking about individuals who persevere. For example, figure skating champions Kurt Browning and Elvis Stojko have demonstrated repeatedly, despite injuries, the will to become a champion.

Promoting perseverance through children's literature

Earrings, by Judith Viorst, is the story of a young girl who uses various arguments to convince her parents to let her have her ears pierced. The number of times she asks her parents the same question and the numerous strategies she uses to change her parents' minds provide a model for understanding perseverance.

Once you have read *Earrings* to the whole class, invite students to reflect upon a current problem with their parents and to think of about three strategies they might use to sway their parents' minds. Select some students to dramatize the problem and the strategies used to change the situation or issue. Have students use criteria that they have set to evaluate the degree of perseverance demonstrated in the scenario.

The Wednesday Surprise, by Eve Bunting, is a great story to read and discuss to provide a greater understanding of what it means to show perseverance. Everyone thinks that on Wednesday nights Grandma is teaching her grandchild, Anna, to read. But it's Anna teaching Grandma, a difficult task. Both Anna and Grandma demonstrate perseverance.

After reading this story out loud, you might ask students to think about a time they had to use great willpower to learn how to do something, for example, riding a bicycle. Have students trace the ups and downs of their experience, then share the summary with another student.

Unravelling mysteries

Dugald Steer puts perseverance as a personal trait up front and centre in his challenging, interactive book, *Mythical Mazes*. Steer creates a collection of illustrated labyrinths that cast individuals in the roles of some of the great characters of legend. Students are asked to unravel the mysteries of each maze.

As a follow-up, you can ask students to work in small cooperative learning groups to create mazes of their own. Have each group present its maze using an overhead projector and challenge another group to unravel the mystery. Record the time a group begins and ends work on the task.

Most puzzles require a stick-to-it frame of mind and can be used in the classroom for strengthening perseverance.

The perseverance of inventors

Albert Einstein's stubborn relentless pursuit of the truth forever changed humankind's view of the universe. Invite students to use the Internet to find out about another inventor who demonstrates perseverance. Ask students how they might go about strengthening this trait in themselves. Suggest that they create a mind map using pictures and words to illustrate their thoughts.

The influence of perseverance on lifelong learning

Mastering any skill requires practice and practice demands perseverance. To acquire and strengthen any of the lifelong learning skills, students must develop the staying power that comes from within. Otherwise, they will founder. As would any of us.

The Influence of Personal Traits on Lifelong Learning

Each of the seven traits identified in my Portrait of Lifelong Learning is essential to individual and group survival. Perhaps, what their absence would mean best points to this. To be void of curiosity in the 21st century would signifiy a loss of discovery, resulting in reduced innovation and slower progress. Without imagination the world as we have known it would come to a standstill. Without initiative the status quo would prevail. Lack of flexibility and adaptability would limit the opportunities we can provide for students. Unless we accept responsibility for our own learning — and persevere in its pursuit — we cannot enter the lifelong learning culture.

CHAPTER FOUR
. . . .

Communication Skills

I found it on the Internet is now a far more powerful
statement than I was reading a book the other day . . .
Robert Everett Green, "The Growth of Magic in a
Technological World," *Toronto Star*

The information and communication revolution has resulted in
unlimited information exchange and a globalized communication
system. In this new globalized economy, learning to speak and
write more than one language is a significant part of functioning
in a lifelong learning culture. Change is happening quickly due to
the accelerated flow of information, and as Microsoft chief Bill
Gates says in *The Road Ahead*, the major changes are coming in the
way people communicate with each other.

The way students work with information is changing too. For
example, science teacher Tan Wah Chin is involved in a pilot
project that will see teacher and students interacting via computer.
Multimedia lessons will come alive on computer screens with
moving images, words, and sounds. Students will plug into their
school's network from home, do their research, and hand in assign-
ments without putting pen to paper ("Opening Up New Vistas in
Class Through Teaching by Computer," *International News*).

The Five Forms of Language

Computer literacy is only one of the skills needed for survival in
the new knowledge-based economy. Robert K. Logan, in *The Fifth
Language*, notes that these skills are developed within a new form
of language — computing. Teachers can use computer technologies to support instruction in various kinds of communication, for

34

example, software to support brainstorming. Educators must have facility in computing and continue to build on the skills inherent in all other forms of language: speech, writing, math, and science. Speech permeates all other language forms, including a variety of communication vehicles (e.g., distance learning). Writing provides opportunities for students to express thoughts, feelings, and opinions; explore ideas and experiences; and inform, describe, and explain — these characteristics are embedded in all five forms of language. Mathematics is a means of communication too. Students are charged with expressing their ideas clearly while mastering basic skills and solving problems. As well, communication in science can take various shapes. Students may take part in related class or group discussions, use manipulative materials, or keep a journal to communicate their learning.

Communication skills have evolved over time and remain interconnected, beginning with oral language and continuing to computing. With the introduction of this new language form, the role of language has changed. It now goes beyond communication to include information processing; we use language to communicate, store, retrieve, organize, and process information. Each language form processes information differently; for example, graphs can represent our learning.

In communicating children develop and consolidate their communication skills: listening, speaking, reading, writing, viewing, and presenting. These skills can be practised in numerous ways. The flow chart on the next page identifies the five language forms noted earlier and the communication skills inherent in all forms of language. The communication vehicles, such as personal contact and books, allow appropriate communication to take place. Teachers can provide the necessary encouragement and support students need to develop their communication skills by creating opportunities to practise these skills.

In this chapter, I will introduce each communication skill and provide an insight web for each and sample activities that enable students to develop their communication skills within the five forms of language. Teachers may perhaps go on to design their own activities, using the format outlined in Aids to Building Communication Skills in the Classroom (see page 45). I will conclude by putting into context the new role of language.

Developing Classroom Activities to Build Communication Skills

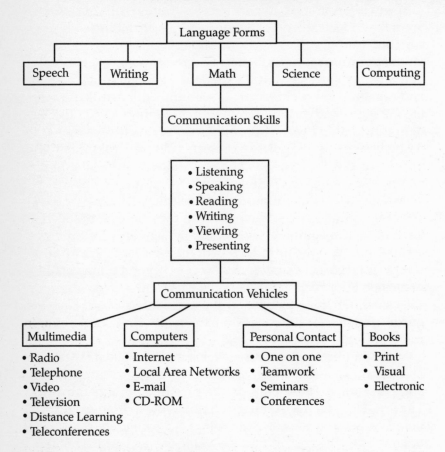

Building Listening Skills

Good listeners can identify issues, understand directions, obtain information, and exchange ideas more readily

We need to provide opportunities for students to develop their listening skills throughout the five forms of language. As an integral part of communication, listening skills are fully transferable and require practice. We also need to practise our own listening skills. In *The Meaning Makers*, Gordon Wells advises teachers to "talk less and listen more. Allow students longer time to think out what they want to say and give them time to say it without interruption."

Listening: An Insight Web

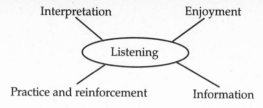

SPEECH: Invite students to listen to a read-aloud story, perhaps recommended in Jim Trelease's *Read-Aloud Handbook*. Make your selection from a variety of genres representing our diverse society. If you read aloud *The Eleventh Hour* by Graeme Base, for example, ask students to listen for the clues to who stole the food for the birthday banquet. Invite some students to share the clues orally. Students can then work in groups, creating their own questions in response to the text. They can extend their learning by sharing the questions orally with the class. (L1)

WRITING: Read a story with a problem embedded in the text. One example is *King Bidgood's in the Bathtub* by Audrey Wood. Encourage students to listen to the story to identify the problem — in this case, the king's refusal to leave the tub to govern his kingdom. In small groups, students should discuss and record their ideas about how the problem might have been solved differently. (L2)

MATH: Take students on a walk through a busy part of town. Ask them to listen to all the sounds there and to record what they might be. Students should count the number of times they heard similar sounds. You might then let them represent their numerical data using computer software to create a bar graph or arrange the data into a chart. A bar graph appears below. (L3)

Sounds Heard in the Community

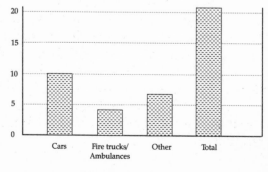

SCIENCE: Encourage students to listen to and record a variety of sounds (for example, birds, cars, insects, and airplanes) in their environment. Have students compare their sounds and discuss how some of the sounds may contribute to noise pollution. (L4)

COMPUTING: Use software such as Sitting on the Farm, available on CD-ROM and distributed by Sanctuary Woods. Engage students in the learning activities which include listening, reading along, writing about, and recording. (L5)

Building Speaking Skills

"The ability to express an idea is well nigh as important as the idea itself," Bert Decker notes in *The Art of Communicating*. Whether in daily dialogue or in formal public settings, speaking skills are much in demand in business and the community. Useful resources for developing students' verbal skills include *Speak Up! Speak Out!*, by Bob and Barbara Greenwood; and *Effective Presentation Skills* and *Technical Presentation Skills*, both by Steve Mandel.

Speaking: An Insight Web

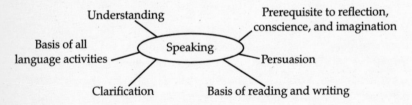

SPEECH: Provide a few minutes for each student to talk to the class about their favorite book. Refer students to *Speak Up! Speak Out!* for tips on speaking. As the book says, "If you only have a few minutes, you have to get right to the point." Using this resource, have students set the speaking criteria for the talks, for example, tone of voice, word choice. As each student speaks, the rest of the class should rank the talk according to the set criteria. (S1)

WRITING: Invite students to write their own poetry using rhyme, rhythm, and other word patterns. They can then read their poems aloud to students in another class. (S2)

MATH: Read *Grandfather Tang's Story*, by Ann Tompart, to the class. Once students have seen how Tompart uses tangrams to show the characters' shapes, ask them, in small groups, to manipulate tangrams to reproduce the tangram puzzles set out in the story. Invite each small group to create a tangram puzzle and present it to the class. (S3)

SCIENCE: Tell students to conduct their own experiment in relation to an area of study. Ask them to express orally the step-by-step procedure required to do the experiment. (S4)

COMPUTING: Use two microphones, one for the sender and one for the receiver, and appropriate hardware and software. Invite pairs of students to conduct a two-way conversation on a topic of interest. (S5)

Building Reading Skills

Students need to see reading as a lifelong activity, not just something they do in school. As educators we must provide opportunities for them to develop their reading skills throughout the language forms. They need opportunities to gather and process information, develop opinions, and make connections between school and the outside world. That's because everything in our man-made environment depends on our ability to read and reading skills are linked to thinking and problem-solving skills.

Reading: An Insight Web

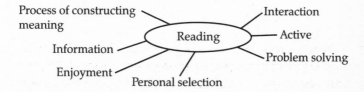

SPEECH: Invite students to read several different versions of the same children's story, for example, The Three Little Pigs. Alternative versions include *The True Story of the Three Little Pigs* by Jon Scieszka and *The Three Little Wolves and the Big Bad Pig* by Eugene Trivizas. Provide each group with a different version of the story. Allow time for a student from each group to present orally a synopsis of their version. Ask students to compare the stories, creating a class chart of the similarities and differences of each. (R1)

WRITING: Teach students how to access information from the Internet. As a safety precaution, bookmark Internet articles that are specific to the unit of study. Challenge the students to use the Internet to locate a journal article that will help them in the study of the unit. Instruct them to pull the article off the Internet and to write a short note on the focus of the article. (R2)

MATH: Using *The 13th Clue*, by Ann Jonas, you can involve students in the use of critical and creative thinking and problem-solving strategies. (See the next two chapters.) Read the story aloud, then have students work in groups to unscramble the codes. (R3)

SCIENCE: Tell students to choose a manufactured product, such as Velcro. They should research its origin and use(s), using the Internet. Invite them to present their findings to the class. (R4)

COMPUTING: Use software such as What's My Story, available on CD-ROM and distributed by Brøderbund. Invite students to read the interactive story. To extend their learning, encourage them to create their own stories, weaving film clips and sounds from the stories they've heard into their own.

Students may use the software package HyperStudio, by Roger Wagner Publishing, to create interactive and creative products. HyperStudio provides templates for developing animated cards with sound effects. As well, it allows students to create school projects, portfolios, interactive games, and written and illustrated books. (R5)

Building Writing Skills

We can use and extend our writing skills throughout our lifetimes. Skills such as organizing and developing ideas logically and choosing words, phrases, and structures that are appropriate for the context are developed through practice. Writing clarifies our thoughts and enables us to engage in critical thinking in school, the workplace, and the community. As French novelist Jean Malaquais writes, "The only time I know that something is true is at the moment I discover it in the act of writing." We need to provide opportunities for students to develop their writing skills throughout the various forms of language. One useful reference is Kathy Stinson's *Writing Your Best Picture Book Ever*.

Writing: An Insight Web

SPEECH: Display poetry books randomly about the classroom. Share a variety of poems orally with the class. Ask students to create their own poems and read them to the class. Combine poems into a big book of poetry for others to read. (W1)

WRITING: Adopting the buddy system, have older and younger students work together to create their own stories. Let them follow the writing process through to the publishing stage, then put children's stories on display in the library for others to read. (W2)

MATH: Read aloud children's stories that focus on developing number concepts: Olivier Dunrea's *Deep Down Underground* is one. Have students each create a big book of numbers from 1–10. Share with younger students in other classes. (W3)

SCIENCE: Invite students to choose a science instrument, such as a magnifying glass, prism, or kaleidoscope, from a mystery box. Encourage them to write an adventure story, in the first person, using the object as an integral component of the plot. (W4)

COMPUTING: Use software such as Amazing Writing Machine, available in CD-ROM and distributed by Brøderbund. Invite students to express their thoughts, ideas, and opinions in a written form of their choice: story, letter, poem, or journal. (W5)

Building Viewing Skills

It is important to provide opportunities for students to develop their viewing skills throughout the various forms of language. Since we are bombarded daily with photographs, videos, digital images, and illustrations, we need to understand such visual imagery which may enhance our quality of life. Children learn by seeing. Research indicates 80 percent of the learning in the first 12 years of life comes from visual stimulation. Visual literacy can be developed in a number of ways. For example, photography, as a tool for communication, provides a rich new language for sharing ideas. "A picture is worth a thousand words" holds true when you observe young children's reliance on pictures. You can use Polaroid's *Visual Learning Guide and Activity Book* to enhance your students' viewing skills.

Viewing: An Insight Web

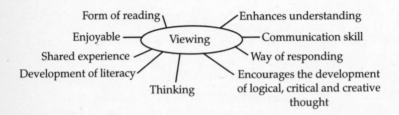

SPEECH: Show students a video on a curriculum topic. Tell them to write, cooperatively, a synopsis of the key points. They can then record their written response, using a tape recorder, and share it with the rest of the class. (V1)

WRITING: Use Kid Works 2, available in CD-ROM and distributed by Davidson. Encourage students to create and illustrate their own stories. Have them use the computer to read the stories back to them. Students will thereby learn to express themselves visually and in writing. (V2)

MATH: Let students observe and explore two- and three-dimensional geometric shapes. They can use their knowledge, as well as hands-on materials, to create models integrating as many of the shapes as possible. Put models on display in the school, challenging the students to observe, sort and classify, and record the number of different shapes used to construct the models. (V3)

SCIENCE: Introduce the software Incredible Machine, available in CD-ROM and distributed by Sierra. Students can construct cause-and-effect contraptions with working pulleys, levers, conveyor belts and more, always solving different puzzles. Encourage students to build their own puzzles in the blank template provided within the software package. (V4)

COMPUTING: Let students view a video clip on how to make kites, a popular activity in some parts of the world. Next, set them up with a draw package on the computer to design their own kite patterns. Invite students to put their patterns to the test by building the actual kite. (V5)

Building Presenting Skills

Bearing in mind that presentation methods change and grow as the world evolves, we must seek to provide opportunities for students to develop their presenting skills. As they do so throughout the various forms of language, they will need to know how to use current technology such as digital imagery.

Presenting: An Insight Web

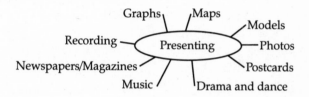

SPEECH: Ask students to bring their favorite postcard to class. Have them project it on a screen and share orally what makes it their favorite. Follow up with student questions and discussion. (P1)

WRITING: Show students TV commercials in preparation for a project in which they will create their own commercials to enhance their audio-visual skills. Invite outside expertise into the classroom to facilitate a hands-on video camera workshop. Teach about the key elements of successful commercials, for example, time and pace. Ask students, in groups, to write their own commercials for a product of their choice and to record it using a video camera. Let them view their commercials. (P2)

MATH: Use TesselMania, available in CD-ROM and distributed by MECC, to let students create tessellations, formed through the manipulation of small squares resulting in the creation of intricate patterns. Allow students to showcase their tessellations as posters, stationery, calendars, and 3-D objects. (P3)

SCIENCE: You could use April Wilson's *Look Again!*, a wordless book illustrating the ecosystems in our world. Select five different focused areas for students to explore. In small groups, students should choose their area of study, for example, "The Jungles of Central America." Students are challenged to use their observation skills and thinking skills to identify the 12 differences between a pair of pictures that, at first glance, look identical. Invite each group to present its findings to the whole class. (P4)

COMPUTING: Invite students to use a draw package on the computer to create their own patterns. Have them print out their patterns using a color printer and display them on a bulletin board for all to see. (P5)

Providing Varied Opportunities for Practice

Here are two examples of educators calling upon students to practise a variety of communication skills, using some of the five forms of language where appropriate.

My son Jonathan, as a teacher candidate, designed a unit on animal coverings, such as skin and fur, for the Grade 1 students in his charge. He began with three goals in mind:

- to use as many of the five forms of language as possible
- to provide opportunities for the students to share their learning through the use of speaking, reading, writing, viewing, and presenting
- to use the computer to enhance their learning

Jonathan taught the students how to use a draw package. He then encouraged them to use this software to draw an animal of their choice. Next, they used their keyboarding skills to input the letters of the word that would identify their animal, and presented their digital images, which were projected by an LCD panel onto a large screen. The follow-up discussion provided many opportunities for students to practise listening, speaking, reading, writing, viewing, and presenting.

Information is processed very differently in a program in math and science developed by the Ontario-based group, Mariposa in the Schools. Facilitators involve students in songs and stories to teach such basics as estimation, the scientific method, and the workings of simple machines. On one occasion, storyteller Sally Jagar told an animal tale to explain the principle of a fulcrum to Grade 1 students. Mariposa consultant Joseph Romain commented, "When these students get into Grade 3 and learn the fulcrum they'll imagine the turtle wedged underneath the rock. They'll remember the meaning — and that's what learning is about" ("Teaching Children to Learn," in the *Why* Spring 1996 issue).

Aids to Building Communication Skills in the Classroom

Since education relies on communication, you may want to develop activities to enhance your students' language skills in all areas of learning in your classroom. Some aids are outlined below.

Classroom activity planning

A Communication Skills and Strategies Planning Chart can help you plan a balanced program in the communication skills. My chart codes activities by using the first letter of each communication skill plus a number between 1 and 5 to indicate the language form used. For example, L1 is a listening skill activity using speech.

A Communication Skills and Strategies Planning Chart

COMMUNICATION SKILLS	LANGUAGE FORMS				
	1 SPEECH	2 WRITING	3 MATH	4 SCIENCE	5 COMPUTING
Listening (L)	L1	L2	L3	L4	L5
Speaking (S)	S1	S2	S3	S4	S5
Reading (R)	R1	R2	R3	R4	R5
Writing (W)	W1	W2	W3	W4	W5
Viewing (V)	V1	V2	V3	V4	V5
Presenting (P)	P1	P2	P3	P4	P5

The chart can be used in many ways. Teachers may find it useful to begin with a blank template and when planning a unit of study, for example, math, fill in the communication skill(s) to be emphasized during the unit of work. The chart could also serve as a record used throughout the year to determine a balance in activities developed within any integrated unit of work.

Children's literature as a forum for skill development

Lifelong Learning Skills uses this strategy extensively. Children's literature can build communication skills, demonstrate higher order thinking skills, and provide opportunities for the development of problem-solving skills, critical and creative thinking skills, and interpersonal skills. The flexible web on page 47, "Building Communication Skills Through Children's Literature," features children's books organized into categories representing the five forms of language. Children's literature is an invaluable tool for developing, enhancing, and enriching lifelong literacy.

Computer software

This chapter mentions a variety of CD-ROM programs designed to strengthen information literacy skills.

Communication Skills in a Lifelong Learning Context

The nature of communication is changing drastically. With its role expanded to cover information processing, communication now involves analyzing, manipulating, and storing information. It is thereby becoming more complex, something that is reflected in the recognition of computing as a fifth language form. More than ever, students need to become information literate (see "Information Literacy and Lifelong Learning" on page 19 in Chapter 2). They need to develop the flexibility to communicate in an increasing variety of ways: not just through personal contact (ranging from one on one to conferences) and books (including print, visual, and electronic) but through computers — the Internet, E-mail, CD-ROMs, and local area networks — and multimedia vehicles (including radio and teleconferences). Amidst this flux, the skills themselves — listening, speaking, reading, writing, viewing, and presenting — are readily transferable and in demand.

Building Communication Skills Through Children's Literature

Children's Literature

Speech

- Til All the Stars Have Fallen
- Primary Rhymerry
- Wacky Word Games
- Speak Up! Speak Out!
- Many Luscious Lollipops
- A Cache of Jewels
- The Merry-Go-Round Dog
- Kites Sail High
- The Icky Bug
- Brainstorm!

Writing

- Wacky Word Games
- Brainstorm!
- The Best Picture Book Ever

Math

- Mr. Archimedes' Bath
- From Map to Museum
- The Eleventh Hour
- How Many Snails?
- Math Curse
- Brainstorm!
- Grandfather Tang's Story

Science

- The Technology of Materials
- How to Think Like a Scientist
- Peterson First Guides
- Science Mini-Mysteries
- Brainstorm!
- How Far Will a Rubber Band Stretch?
- June 29, 1999

Computing

- Let's Look at Computers
- Internet for Kids
- Every Student's Guide to the Internet
- Kidnet

Here is an extended list of children's fiction and nonfiction titles presented under the five forms of language.

CHAPTER FIVE

Critical and Creative Thinking Skills

We do not teach how to think. This is a very serious
failure that may even compromise the human future.
Carl Sagan, quoted in "The Thinking Gap"
in *Vital Connections*

As Ron Brandt wrote in a 1986 *Educational Leadership* article, the
thinking that young children do prior to entering school and that
which practising scientists and artists do is more similar than
anything that goes on in between. Yet thinking is the foundation
of learning and can be taught.

Thinking for Themselves

As educators we must strive to produce individuals able to think
for themselves and not merely follow someone else. Students
need to develop proficiency in key thinking skills so that they can
cope with a wide variety of thinking challenges. To further this,
we need to teach them how to identify and conceptualize problems, generate and evaluate alternative solutions, generate new
ideas and products, and more. If students learn higher level
thinking skills, such as interpreting and inferring, they can effectively solve the problems they encounter throughout their lives.

Our challenge is to engage students in tasks requiring the kinds
of thinking we want them to develop. For example, we may ask
students to compare and contrast two ideas and point out that
they are practising analysis. To meet this challenge, we need to

become cognizant of the thinking skills we are developing and share this information with the students so that they may learn and grow in applying these thinking skills. We must also acquire an understanding and appreciation of the skills' ongoing value and use throughout their lives. In our unpredictable world, we will all need to think about more decisions, plans, initiatives, and choices than ever before.

Critical and creative thinking skills, both recognized in my Portrait of Lifelong Learning, overlap in a thinking environment whose characteristics are outlined below. These skills can be considered two sides of the same coin: while the four basic components of creative products are flexibility, originality, fluency, and elaboration (see Creative Thinking Skills on page 53), critical thinking uses the practice in fluency, flexibility, and originality exercises to develop the advanced skills of planning, forecasting, decision making, and evaluation.

Characteristics of a Thinking Environment in the Classroom

There is freedom for supposing.

Thinking skills are introduced separately and integrated in the content areas.

There is a balance of content and process.

Thinking is part of the classroom culture.

Everyone has an opportunity to pose problems and raise questions that may be resolved.

Interaction and dialogue are ongoing.

There is time for reflection.

There is an awareness of the thinking process.

Thinking behaviors are role-modelled throughout the environment.

There is a belief in respect for others.

Students are engaged in thinking tasks that call for hands-on activities.

Each kind of thinking is important to the success of the other, something that Paul Pisek explores in *Creativity, Innovation and Quality*. In his words, "We need the ability to be analytical when the situation calls for it and creative when the situation calls for that." Both skills are crucial for success, the degree and emphasis varying.

Lifelong Learning Skills will explore how the two skills are inter-related, investigate their natures, and provide suggestions for practising, extending, and enhancing critical and creative thinking in the classroom.

The Complementarity of Critical and Creative Thinking Skills

Although critical thinking is often referred to as evaluative and creative thinking as generative, in practice the two types of thinking complement each other. Recognizing that both are needed to maximize thinking, we need to develop a course of action for teaching them. First of all, we must understand the similarities and differences of each skill. The comparison chart developed by the American Association of School Administrators in *Teaching Thinking and Reasoning Skills* is most useful in this regard.

A Comparison of the Natures of Critical and Creative Thinking

Critical thinking	Creative thinking
Is purposeful and dominated by goals	Involves taking risks
Is reasonable and reflective, and focuses on deciding what to believe and what to do	Calls for continual recasting of ideas — creative thinkers are flexible in their approach to tasks
Involves comparing and contrasting information with standards or criteria	Involves intense desire and preparation but uses flashes of insight from the sub-conscious

---

Looking at specific goals that lead to the development of critical and creative thinking for all students also helps to understand the linkages of these two processes. Setting skill-specific thinking goals for students is a useful method for teachers to adopt. I have used the Valley Educational Consortium work, from Oregon, on setting goals as a springboard to understanding goal setting in relation to critical and creative thinking.

Goals for Critical Thinking	Goals for Creative Thinking
The student will be able to draw valid inferences, generalizations, analogies, and conclusions; build logical arguments, explanations, and predictions; evaluate arguments, explanations, and predictions critically.	*The student will be able to* discover meanings and patterns in experiences; view and interpret experiences from a variety of perspectives; draw connections between and integrate two or more bodies of knowledge.

With a clear understanding of these two thinking processes, teachers can plan and develop thinking activities, such as inventing a new toy, that concentrate on developing the higher level mental functions. I set goals for achieving a balance in critical and creative thinking in my classroom. From these goals I develop thinking activities for my students, recognizing that the outcomes will vary depending on whether the task demands critical or creative thinking. I also consciously model these thinking skill processes with my students.

Since good thinking draws on both skills, I will take a closer look at each process.

Critical Thinking Skills

Critical thinking tasks focus on gathering and recalling information, understanding and interpreting information, applying what is learned to new situations to solve problems, analyzing a problem into its component parts, and synthesizing various aspects or components into a new whole to solve problems.

To complete such tasks, students need to learn the appropriate critical thinking skills. Some key ones from a broad spectrum include: using reliable sources; determining cause-and-effect relationships; making valid conclusions; recognizing the details/parts that form a whole; selecting criteria appropriate to judge data; identifying attributes of a person, place or thing; making valid

51

inferences from data; and classifying information and ideas. Teachers should select appropriate skills when planning learning experiences to emphasize critical thinking skills in the classroom.

We think critically when we think our way through a problem to a solution. Doing this involves the use of the reflective and analytical facets of critical thinking. We look at what we are doing and assess how well our solution is working; we also exercise complex reasoning and look at questions from different perspectives.

However, we need to carry our methodology further to include teaching the skills in the context of an area of learning. Research indicates that teaching critical thinking skills in isolation results in little transfer of these skills to other areas of work. We want to ensure that we meet the overall critical thinking goals for students, noted above.

The graphic that follows identifies characteristics of a desirable climate for critical thinking.

Classroom Conditions Conducive to Promoting Critical Thinking

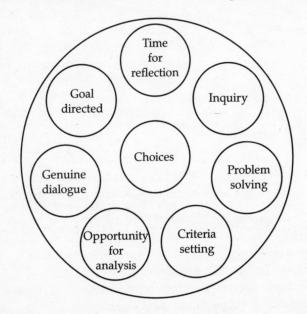

Critical thinking in action

Perhaps the best way to identify the characteristics of critical thinking is through the sharing of a hands-on experience of my

Grade 6 students. My students had been planning various large-group, small-group, and individual activities around a unit on Mexico. A large-group activity they decided to undertake was the building of a life-size Mexican kiosk. They brainstormed all the jobs that would be necessary to effectively carry out the plan, then formed small working groups based on their interests. One group researched and recorded the necessary information on Mexican kiosks. Another used graph paper to make a scale design of the kiosk. A third reflected on the drawing and predicted what resources they would need to build the kiosk, how much they would need of certain materials, and what the overall costs would be.

Students had to ponder many problems. For example, they had to figure out how much weight the roof on the kiosk would bear. They planned to use straw for the roof, but had to be sure of the weight and quantity required. Throughout this process, they had many opportunities to think critically, for example, when predicting material quantities from the scale drawing and when discussing the consequences of their actions and alternative solutions to their problems.

Creative Thinking Skills

Divergent thinking, synonymous with creative thinking, is the cornerstone of the creative process. This process has five overlapping stages: preparation, incubation, illumination, evaluation, and elaboration, and it usually begins with the goal of solving a problem. The total creative process is a balance of imagination and analysis. As Paul Pisek puts it, "Imagination and analysis are equal partners in creativity . . . The ability to shape and develop an idea is just as important as the ability to imagine the idea in the first place" (*Creativity, Innovation and Quality*).

As noted earlier, creative products reflect four basic components:

- fluency — generating multiple ideas
- flexibility — generating different ideas
- elaboration — generating detailed ideas
- originality — generating unique ideas

Creative thinking tasks range from generating novel responses and assessing their validity and planning projects to trying to solve

53

unstructured problems. To complete such tasks, students need to develop creative thinking skills, brainstorming, inventing, determining relationships, inferring, generalizing, predicting, hypothesizing, making analogies, and dealing with ambiguity among them. As classroom teachers we must provide many opportunities for students to practise these skills to develop such personal traits as risktaking, tolerance of ambiguity, imagination, and curiosity.

The graphic below identifies characteristics of a climate appropriate for creative thinking.

Classroom Conditions Conducive to Promoting Creative Thinking

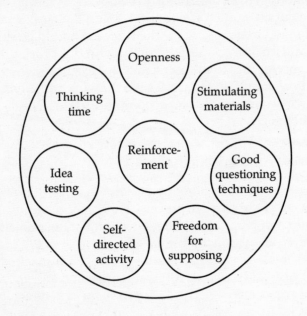

Creative thinking in action

Here is an illustration of creative thinking.

My Grade 5 students had expressed an interest in toys and their movement. We worked as a class to brainstorm on the topic, jotting down what they knew and what they wanted to find out, identifying concepts such as gravity, inertia, friction, force, and balance. Small groups each researched and developed a hands-on experiment to foster a greater understanding of a concept of motion. Then they demonstrated their experiments, one student from each group presenting. To demonstrate inertia, one group spun a spinning top. Students later rotated in their original groups to other stations.

Finally, each student was assigned an independent project. Students, with parental help, were to create working models of toys that would demonstrate understanding of a science concept learned in class. Each student kept a learning log to reflect upon any problems encountered and I provided questions to foster reflection. Also, parents could respond to any of the entries while the project was taking place. One student, Dereck, wrote 10 entries about his efforts to design, cut, glue, and paint a wooden carousel. His ninth entry reads: "The carousel was finished and the only thing left to do was to see if it worked. We spun the carousel and it started to spin."

Fluency, flexibility, elaboration, and originality were demonstrated throughout the activity. Students demonstrated fluency in thinking while brainstorming, a technique also used in the planning and development stages of Dereck's working model. Dereck demonstrated flexibility in thinking in the initial stages of his plan, elaborative thinking through the use of a photo journal which showed changes in detail, and originality in thinking in the manner in which his carousel functioned.

The five stages of the creative process — preparation, incubation, illumination, evaluation, and elaboration — can be traced through Dereck's project. In the preparation stage, Dereck investigated the possibility of making a carousel. He identified what materials he would need and gathered facts on how to go about making a working model. In the incubation stage, Dereck put much thought into how he could go about making his carousel function. The illumination stage saw him put his thoughts together to complete a working model. In the evaluation stage, Dereck tested his model to see if it would work as planned and completed project-specific questions on the process and product. For the elaboration stage, Dereck could add to or build upon the structure of his working model.

Building Critical and Creative Thinking Skills

We need to provide many opportunities for students to develop these important skills. As for other lifelong learning skills, children's literature offers teachers a way to help students develop both critical and creative thinking skills. The teacher's role is to guide students' critical responses to literature by encouraging them to ask questions, confirm predictions, draw inferences, and connect ideas in a storyworld of imagination and exploration. Making personal connections to characters, recalling other versions of a story, and explaining how the sequence of events in one story is similar to that of another serve as opportunities to engage students in the higher level thinking processes. Since not all children's books facilitate this, be sure to choose books carefully. Several good titles are identified in this chapter.

Promoting critical thinking skills through children's literature

Stories provide a natural framework for structuring experiences that facilitate intellectual development, expansion, and refinement. In this environment, students have opportunities to analyze, hypothesize, reflect upon, and process information.

1. In *Mr. Archimedes' Bath*, by Pamela Allen, Mr. Archimedes asks repeatedly, "Can anyone tell me where all this water came from?" Until he explores displacement in his tub with his friends Kangaroo, Wombat, and Goat, his bath always overflows. This story lends itself to teaching the steps of the scientific method. It also allows students to practise specific thinking skills, for example, determining cause and effect through their investigation of the property of buoyancy.
2. Critical thinking opportunities are embedded in *Mrs. Toggle and the Dinosaur*, by Robin Pulver. When a new student arrives, Mrs. Toggle and her class, who are expecting a dinosaur, are surprised. Mrs. Toggle learns to take her own good advice: If you don't understand something the first time you hear it, ask questions. This story allows classes to discuss questioning techniques. Be sure to provide opportunities for students to practise developing good questions.

Promoting creative thinking skills through children's literature

Children's literature can help students develop an appreciation of the creativity of others and encourage them to be more creative in their own efforts.

1. *I Spy: An Alphabet in Art*, by Lucy Micklethwait, takes children on a journey through art masterpieces dating from the Renaissance to modern times. The visual story formed by the paintings stimulates students' imaginations as they compare the painting styles to the methods used to create the paintings. Asking questions such as What do you think he was trying to say? can promote higher level thinking skills.
2. Ruth Heller's imaginative book *Many Luscious Lollipops* provides a stimulus for creative expression. It features playful verse to introduce adjectives and how they are used. It also introduces the creative thinking skill of attributing (discussed further under "Stimulating specific kinds of thinking through special techniques" on page 61) and demonstrates its use.

More Thinking Opportunities in Children's Literature

Critical Thinking

· *Gobley for Mayor!*, by Judi Gamble and Robert McConnell (Toronto: Napoleon, 1991)

· *Tricky Tortoise*, by Mwenye Hadithi and Adrienne Kennaway (London: Hodder, 1990)

· *Math Curse*, by Jon Scieszka and Lane Smith (New York: Viking Children's Books, 1995)

· *June 29, 1999*, by David Wiesner (New York: Clarion Books, 1992)

· *Zoom Upstream*, by Tim Wynne-Jones (Toronto: Groundwood, 1992)

Creative Thinking

· *Window*, by Jeannie Baker (New York: Greenwillow, 1991)

· *Something from Nothing*, by Phoebe Gilman (Richmond Hill, ON: Scholastic, 1992)

· *The Rose in My Garden*, by Arnold Lobel (New York: Greenwillow, 1984)

· *Just a Dream*, by Chris Van Allsburg (Boston: Houghton Mifflin, 1990)

· *Free Fall*, by David Wiesner (New York: Morrow, 1991)

· *Zoom at Sea*, by Tim Wynne-Jones (Toronto: Groundwood, 1990)

3. Another strong title for setting students' imaginations free is Anthony Browne's *Through the Magic Mirror*. When Toby puts out his hand to touch the mirror, he walks right through it onto the street, but nothing is quite as it should be . . . You can encourage students to visualize an aspect of the story and share the vision with a partner.

Using computer software to promote critical thinking skills

Students can use the computer as a way to foster higher level thinking skills and as a resource for solving problems. The best computer software incorporates learning how to use the computer as well as allowing students to explore the software's usefulness. Teachers are encouraged to challenge learners to work with concepts, puzzles, and various computer activities independently.

Students will develop higher level thinking skills as they go about learning the processes of working with databases, spreadsheets, and graphics programs. For example, in constructing a database, students will need to establish the limits of a research project, think through the nature of the information to be sought, design appropriate data collection procedures such as questionnaires and interview schedules, record and classify collected information, organize that information according to an agreed-upon classification system, test hypotheses and make predictions, make inferences, and draw conclusions from the data. Databases help learners sort through information efficiently according to specific categories they can establish for themselves.

1. The Cruncher, by Davidson, introduces children from five to eight to spreadsheets and features a library of animated illustrations and sound effects. There are also tutorials with step-by-step lessons in various tasks.
2. Corel DRAW, by Corel Corporation, allows users to create 3-D objects, slide shows, and other illustrations. The drawing program includes a CD-ROM with many fonts and clip art images.

Developing critical thinking skills through CD-ROMs

All CD-ROMs do not foster higher level thinking skills, so take care when making your selections. Here are a few good ones.

1. MayaQuest, by MECC, lets students act as detectives and explorers searching for answers to explain the collapse of the ancient Mayan civilization. Using it builds research, decision-making, and analytical skills.
2. Sammy's Science House, by Edmark, guides students through a world of science and experimentation in five activities. Students can develop the scientific skills of observation, classification, comparison, sequencing, and problem solving.
3. Edmark's Thinkin' Things 1 helps students to think analytically and solve problems creatively in their quest to become successful learners. Students build thinking skills essential to many disciplines, including math, science, reading, music, and art.

Developing creative thinking skills through CD-ROMs

1. The highly motivating Storybook Weaver Deluxe, by MECC, features state-of-the-art graphics and realistic sound effects. Students can choose from hundreds of images from the folklore of many cultures when they write creatively.
2. In Imagination Express: Oceans, by Edmark, students create their own interactive stories using the detailed scenes in the software. As they do so, they learn about ocean habitats, the role of oceans in ecosystems, and human impact on oceans.
3. In Sierra's Incredible Machine Version 3.0, student inventors learn to construct cause-and-effect contraptions with working pulleys, levers, motors, and more. They use their ingenuity to solve different puzzles, and in a Free Form area, they can expand their creativity further by building their own puzzles.

At my school some students are using HyperStudio, by Wagner, to create multimedia projects. Since students are reading and gathering information from multimedia sources more and more, it may soon be time for them to deliver their research in the same style.

Using hands-on devices to foster thinking

Games, puzzles, and construction materials, such as Lego, foster the development of higher level thinking skills. While manipulating a wide variety of materials, students have many opportunities to think both critically and creatively to solve problems. Working with hands-on devices also helps bring fun to learning, something that I observed through the widespread adoption of Abalone, a strategy board game which combines the skills of Chinese checkers and chess, played cooperatively at my school.

3-D Games: These are brain teasers to sharpen students' thinking skills, and problem-solving skills, too. Dominoes is a familiar example. Besides encouraging dialogue, they present challenging and entertaining problems that can be explored alone, in groups, or at home. Most often they sharpen spatial perception and reasoning skills.

In Zen Blocks, a cube game by Family Pastimes, symbols are matched on the blocks to form a cube, like dominoes in 3-D. The advantage of using Zen Blocks is that it is not a one-solution puzzle but a game that unfolds differently every time. It allows students to demonstrate their intuitiveness and practise higher level thinking skills.

Mind Twister, by Dr. Toyz, is another 3-D game. Colors and numbers are combined into countless formations intricately woven and presented in the shape of a ball. Players must demonstrate openmindedness and imagination as they arrange the numbered tiles of the Wisdom Ball in special numeric or color-coded patterns in the shortest time possible. You might encourage them to create their own game too.

Tantrix, from Tantrix Games in New Zealand, consists of six solitaire puzzles made from hexagonal tiles arranged in unique combinations of green, blue, red, and yellow. Students choose one color, then try to form a continuous closed loop of that color using all 10 Tantrix tiles. The goal is to ensure that the loop goes through all the tiles with this color and that all the other colors match.

Card Games: With the game SET, by Marsha Falco, students can test their reasoning powers. The object of this card game is to identify sets of three cards. Each card is unique in its four features of number, symbols, shading, and color. A SET consists of three cards on which every feature is either the same on all of the cards, or different on all of the cards. Once students have practised playing this visual perception game, they may want to work in small groups to make up a similar game for others to play. Blank cards are easily accessible.

Board Games: Games such as Explorers and Space Future, both by Family Pastimes, allow students to engage in decision making and higher level thinking skills in a natural and entertaining way. In Explorers, students take part in the journeys of such adventurers as Marco Polo, Sir Francis Drake, and James Cook. They choose a journey, make preparations, assemble crews, and venture forth. In Space Future, a team of space explorers undertakes a dangerous mission in which each player has an important role and must return safely to earth. As a follow-up to either game, students could work in groups to create their own board games.

Puzzles: Whether they be from books such as Jenny Lynch's *Mind-Bending Classic Logic Puzzles* or Dan Gilbert's triangular-shaped Wetlands, puzzles call upon higher level thinking skills. Gilbert goes beyond challenging puzzle enthusiasts to work with triangular-shaped pieces to form a large triangle. Once they have pieced together the puzzle, they must search for five things on it that are different from the picture shown on the box cover.

Construction Materials: Ramagon, Lego, Dacta, Duplo, Octoplay, and more enhance students' thinking skills and boggle their imaginations. Once when my class was studying explorers and I had provided students with the option of choosing the method and materials that they felt would best demonstrate their learning, a tactile learner chose Lego. He decided to build a boat representative of the time period we were studying. In preparation for this event he researched the period to ensure authenticity, made a drawing of the boat to scale, predicted how many Lego pieces and what type he would require, and set off to complete the task. In an exercise such as this, students naturally use all of their thinking abilities. After observing the process and product in this instance, I decided to make construction materials an integral part of my classroom program.

Stimulating specific kinds of thinking through special techniques

Some of the most common techniques used to stimulate thinking follow. A closer look at each will uncover strategies specific to individual thinking processes. For example, brainstorming generates fluency in thinking. Once learned, these techniques are transferable to the home, workplace, community, and society.

1. Brainstorming is a group method of generating a quantity of ideas in a short period of time. A good way to begin is to introduce a unique object into the classroom and have students

come up with as many ideas as they can about it. Here are some rules of brainstorming to follow: accept all ideas, welcome the unusual, aim for quantity, suspend judgment, and build and combine with old ideas. Shimkofsky takes an in-depth look at the technique in *Brainstorm!*

2. P.M.I. (Plusses and Minuses of Ideas) is an evaluation technique used by Edward de Bono (see "De Bono's six thinking hats," next chapter). Students are guided into identifying the plusses, minuses, and interesting or important features of something, perhaps a class trip. To provide practice in such analysis, I ask students to bring an unusual object into the classroom and examine its advantages, disadvantages, and interesting points.

3. SCAMPER increases flexibility of thoughts and ideas. The technique's purpose is twofold: to regenerate old material and to view a problem from a different angle. SCAMPER represents a number of ways someone can approach a problem: Substitute, Combine, Adjust, Magnify, Put to other uses, Eliminate/Elaborate, Reverse/Rearrange. The value of this technique is more meaningful to students when it is introduced as part of the brainstorming process or when they are stuck in their thinking.

4. Attributing, a critical thinking tool, promotes a clearer view of the qualities, characteristics, limitations and attributes of a problem. It breaks the problem into its component parts, making the task of solving it seem less overwhelming. Attributing involves listing and labelling things and clarifying facts into categories for quick comparison making. When graphic organizers such as webs, Venn diagrams, and matrices are used, the information is easily accessed.

5. New and alternative approaches, insights, and ideas can often be generated by posing the question What is it like? You can encourage students to draw analogies between their feelings and objects or situations. For example: How would you feel if you were a drop of water under a microscope? Making analogies is useful in identifying perceived relationships between and among symbols, words, and patterns. Solving pattern and word puzzles that focus on developing this skill is a good place to begin. Students can consider how two items relate to each other, then find more that are related in the same way. For example: Tiger Woods / golf; Wayne Gretzky / hockey.

Critical and Creative Thinking Skills in a Lifelong Learning Context

Critical and creative thinking are at the heart of educational reform, and learning and applying these skills should soon be the norm for graduates. Since tomorrow's workplace will demand critical judgment and the quick assimilation of information, students need to develop the thinking skills that will enable them to acquire and process information within a growing field of knowledge. They need to internalize these thinking processes and transfer them to other subjects and life experiences. In a climate of lifelong learning, we must ask ourselves the question Are we, as educators, willing to become critical and creative thinkers role-modelling what our students must internalize and become? The bottom line is If conditions are conducive to thinking, then thinking will take place.

....

CHAPTER SIX

Problem-Solving Skills

The whole process of education should be conceived
as the process of learning to think through the
solution of real problems.

John Dewey

Researchers in the field identify the following elements common
to problem solving: a series of steps, usually starting with a defi-
nition of the problem; a degree of creativity in suggesting possible
solutions; selection of a solution; execution of the solution; and
evaluation of the results.

Working Towards a Goal

No Problem, by Eileen Browne, provides insight into the problem-
solving process. In Browne's story, Mouse receives a big package
filled with bits and pieces waiting to be assembled into a . . . what?
"I can put these together," Mouse says. "No problem." Is it a
bicycle, a car, a boat, an airplane? After many wild guesses Mouse
is in such a hurry that she forgets to look in the box more carefully.
Instead, she decides to work with her friends to fit all of the pieces
together to make a . . . what? After limited success Mouse seeks
the advice of her friend, Shrew. Shrew inquires about what has
been done with the construction materials so far and asks to see
the packing box to see if he can find anything that Mouse might
have overlooked. During his search Shrew discovers the

instructions, reads them over carefully, and follows the steps to build something that really works.

Embodied in Browne's story, and consistent with research presented in *Creating the Thoughtful Classroom*, are these key elements of problem solving: a thinking strategy; use of critical and creative thinking skills; a means of analyzing a situation; a means of applying past experience and knowledge to the problem; a focus on reaching a specific goal; a series of steps in any given model; a recognition that steps are recursive.

The teacher's role throughout the problem-solving process is to foster the development of higher order thinking skills. These skills can be addressed more easily when teachers set goals for problem solving. The goals set down by the American Association of School Administrators in *Teaching Thinking and Reasoning Skills* provide a good place to start. They are, as follows: (1) the student will be able to clarify problems before working towards and implementing solutions; (2) the student will be able to design and implement a plan for solving a problem or deciding upon a course of action; (3) the student will be able to evaluate the adequacy of a problem solution or decision made and respond constructively to evaluation results. Just as Mouse set out with the goal to build something using the construction pieces in a kit, teachers and students will need well-defined personal goals for effective problem solving to take place in the classroom.

Problem-Solving Steps

The problem-solving process involves reaching a specific goal through following a series of steps. There are many different variations of the steps that can be used in the classroom, but they have much in common. Gyorgy Polya, in *How to Solve It*, has a four-step process: understanding the problem, devising a strategy, carrying out the plan, and looking back. John D. Bransford, on the other hand, shares a five-step process which he calls IDEAL. In his process each letter of the word IDEAL represents an individual step. For example: I — Identify the problem; D — Define the problem by thinking about it, sorting out the relevant information and thinking about the root causes; E — Explore solutions by looking at alternatives, brainstorming, and checking out different points of view; A — Act on the strategies; L — Look back and evaluate the effects of your activity (*The Ideal Problem Solver*).

The teacher needs to find a simple method that can be used to teach students the problem-solving process. I have found the steps that Deineka, Hunt, and Pogue outline in *Ages 9 through 12* best for students at the junior level to understand and apply. This Ontario ministry of education resource identifies five steps to the problem-solving process: Visualize, Understand, Organize, Compute, and Evaluate. Each step includes prompts to clarify understanding. For example, Step 1, Visualize, prompts the learner to discuss, draw, restate, and construct. I post the steps in my classroom for the students to reflect upon throughout the year and use as a cueing system.

Sequential Steps to Problem Solving

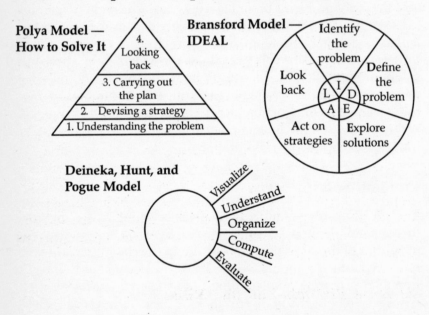

Looking back, sometimes called the "evaluation" stage, or more recently the reflective stage, may be the most important part of problem solving. At this stage students examine the solution by checking the result or argument. They may use the method for some other problem, reinterpret the problem, or restate or state a new problem to solve. If teachers have introduced learning logs, their students may reflect there. I have observed Grade 1 and 2 students using simple learning logs in mathematics to clarify their understanding of the concepts and skills introduced in their class-room learning centres. The consistent use of logs promotes understanding of the concepts for application in the classroom.

When students are provided with a consistent method for solving problems, they generally use the new concepts presented, study their solutions to the problems, and come to a greater personal understanding of the concepts. Teachers can use Browne's *No Problem* to introduce and discuss the steps in the problem-solving process with their students. They can extend its use by organizing students into cooperative learning groups to focus on the following task: to identify, select, record, and present the elements of problem solving as outlined in the story. Students should thereby gain many opportunities to practise higher level thinking skills, such as identifying the key elements of problem solving, classifying and organizing these elements into groups, and interpreting and communicating their results. Opportunities can be further extended for students to practise their social and creative thinking skills, as well as critical thinking skills embedded in problem solving. Teachers may also afford opportunities for students to become involved in planning strategies, anticipating possible consequences, and analyzing their results in a problem-solving world. Students can participate in a whole variety of sequential tasks which may include identifying a general problem, clarifying the problem, formulating hypotheses, formulating appropriate questions, generating related ideas, formulating alternative solutions, choosing the best solution, applying the solution, monitoring acceptance of the solution, and drawing conclusions (*Creating the Thoughtful Classroom*).

Building Problem-Solving Skills

Many methods for the development of problem-solving skills and strategies have been addressed throughout *Lifelong Learning Skills*, and more follow.

Promoting problem-solving and decision-making skills through children's literature

Children's literature can provide a context for a wide variety of experiences for students to learn how to solve problems. Stories provide a vehicle for teaching the sequential steps implicit in the problem-solving process. One of the most powerful motivators for learning is the need for children to seek answers to their own questions, something that children's stories can raise. For example, *Albert's Toothache*, by Barbara Williams, raises interesting questions in metaphysics and the philosophy of mind. Stories promote patterns of cause and effect and problem solution. As well, they provide a model for students to recognize the elements of effective decision making.

1. *The Wretched Stone*, by Chris Van Allsburg, describes how a strange glowing stone picked up on a sea voyage captivates a ship's crew and has a transforming effect on them. The ship's captain, who has been keeping a journal on the voyage, observes the changes and records them. What is this extraordinary rock? What wretched power does it hold? The problem is the strange behavior of the ship's crew; the goal, to find a solution to it.

   Again, teachers might encourage students to keep learning logs to facilitate exploration of situations, events, or issues. Learning logs can provide opportunities for students to pose questions, reflect upon their observations, and pursue possible solutions to problems. Just as the captain in Van Allsburg's story reflected upon journal notes to arrive at a solution to the crew's behavior, students can reflect upon their learning logs to bring about solutions to problems they encounter.

2. In *A Day with Wilbur Robinson*, by William Joyce, Wilbur and his best friend try to find Grandfather Robinson's missing glasses. They come up with a common strategy in their quest to solve the problem, looking for clues inside and outside the house. Developing strategies to solve problems is often seen as a second step in problem solving. Teachers can work with their students on developing strategies to resolve problems effectively by providing students with sample problems to analyze and opportunities to create and discuss strategies for their resolution.

3. The problem in Audrey Wood's *King Bidgood's in the Bathtub* is the king's reluctance to leave the bathtub. The goal is to find a plan to get him out of it. The problem is resolved by the Page when he pulls the plug! Learning to be flexible and to think creatively as demonstrated by the Page are skills exhibited by good problem solvers.

More Problem-Solving Opportunities in Children's Literature

· *Willy the Wimp*, by Anthony Browne (Toronto: Random House of Canada, 1989)

· *The Tunnel*, by Anthony Browne (London, U.K.: Walker Books, 1993)

· *The Tricky Sticky Problem*, by Diana Noonan (New Zealand: Learning Media, 1996)

· *Whizz! Click!*, by Diana Noonan (New Zealand: Learning Media, 1996)

· *Roses Sing on New Snow*, by Paul Yee (Toronto: Groundwood, 1991)

Developing problem-solving skills through CD-ROMs

1. Math Workshop, by Brøderbund, gives students an opportunity to develop and practise critical math skills in a creative environment. By engaging in a variety of fun-filled math activities, students can build effective problem-solving skills, and strategic thinking and computation skills.
2. Thinkin' Things 3, by Edmark, features Stocktopus, an octopus stockbroker, and other friends to challenge students to develop their reasoning abilities, analyze and synthesize information, and build key problem-solving and other critical thinking skills.
3. Sierra's Lost Mind of Dr. Brain stretches problem-solving skills to the limit as students think their way through thousands of puzzles and logic problems. Students are asked to solve brain-building puzzles in 10 game areas.

Integrating Problem-Solving Skills

There are numerous models from which to choose. First, decide what skill you would like to introduce. An easy way to go about this is to base your selection on the needs of your students. Second, find the subject matter that best lends itself to teaching the skill. If, for example, developing a student's ability to make informed and rational decisions is the goal, then considering what skills are involved is critical to effective implementation, in this case, organizing personal questions and interests, doing hands-on investigations, and practising the scientific method. The scientific method is the context in which students can hone their questioning skills and practise hands-on investigations. Through these opportunities students learn and grow to make informed and rational decisions. They follow these sequential steps: ask a question, gather information about the question, form a hypothesis, test the hypothesis, and tell others about discoveries. Teachers can introduce students to activities that stimulate their curiosity and provide opportunities for them to develop and practise these skills so that they will be prepared to make informed and rational decisions throughout their lives.

The problem-solving process will vary according to the kind of problem considered and the strategy the teacher wishes to pursue. For example, in *No Problem* all that was left of the problem-solving process for Shrew was to follow the instructions provided, with little opportunity for him to develop his own thinking. This practice is questionable given our goal to improve students' skills in solving problems.

A familiar method used to promote higher level thinking skills is the interdisciplinary approach to learning. This approach lends itself nicely to integrating the higher level thinking skills across all areas of the curriculum within a problem-solving environment. Since a flood of information on thinking and problem solving exists, I will take only a few moments to touch on Bloom's taxonomy and de Bono's six thinking hats to indicate the usefulness and practicality of these models in the classroom.

Bloom's taxonomy

Bloom's taxonomy is a continuum of thinking skills reflected in six major hierarchical categories: knowledge, comprehension, application, analysis, synthesis, and evaluation. It provides a structured model for teachers and students to learn how to formulate questions at all levels of the taxonomy, strengthening the development of thinking skills in students. Teachers use the different levels to create student activities that integrate both the process and the product to reflect all six levels of the hierarchy. *Those Bloomin' Books: A Handbook for Extending Thinking Skills*, by Carol Kruise, contains a lot of ideas and activities to guide any teacher in developing appropriate higher level thinking activities for their students.

Bloom's Taxonomy

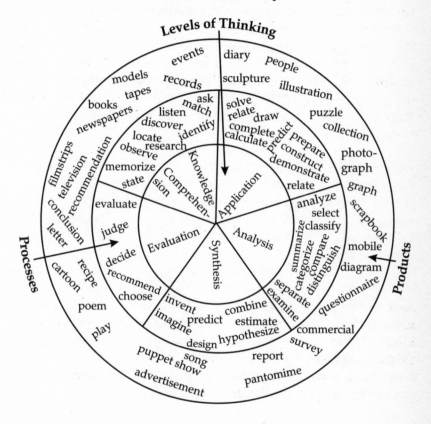

Over the years I have incorporated Bloom's thinking process into the daily classroom experience with much success. I have used it in every subject area across the curriculum and with students ranging from limited ability to students in the Gifted program. My students have learned to formulate their own questions to reflect all levels of the taxonomy and I have grown in expanding my use of this model.

The most recent development, the Q-approach, which my students are still trying to perfect, is outlined in *Cooperative Learning and Higher Level Thinking: The Question Matrix*. It uses Bloom's taxonomy as a partner to help teachers and students formulate higher level questions using the Q-materials. Students and teachers use materials such as Q-dice and Q-dials as motivators to encourage good questioning skills. The objective is to generate questions at all levels. Their most powerful use is in cooperative learning teams where students are empowered to ask higher order questions of one another.

Other models for designing activities according to a hierarchy of skills and behaviors include William's taxonomy of creativity, Krathwohl's taxonomy of affective development, and Gardner's theory of multiple intelligences.

De Bono's six thinking hats

De Bono's six thinking hats, explored in his book of the same name, reflect the various thinking modes we need to apply to a topic. His six colored hats, each representing a different mode of thinking, are highly motivating for students and adults alike. They have a variety of uses throughout the creative thinking cycle.

The Six Thinking Hats	
White	Think about data, facts, information.
Yellow	Think about positives, benefits, good things.
Black (Purple)	Think about negatives, warnings, pitfalls.
Green	Think about creative possibilities and new ideas.
Red	Think about feelings and intuitions.
Blue	Exert control or direction over thinking.

The object of either changing the color of the hat visually or figuratively is to help individuals to focus or redirect their thinking. In the end, de Bono's model encourages individuals to think more productively. The success of his model lies in exploring real-life situations.

A relevant strategy used by my sister, a teacher instructor, included setting a bunch of party hats on a table. She felt her students would enjoy the experience of wearing the different colored hats while she introduced and they applied de Bono's model. Her students enjoyed the experience and learned a lot about the model's application.

Problem-Solving Skills in a Lifelong Learning Context

Since most of us spend more than half of our time solving problems, we need an effective set of problem-solving skills. Lynda Knapp and Allen Glenn share their insights into the characteristics of effective problem solvers in *Restructuring Schools with Technology*. Such problem solvers

- apply a variety of problem-solving strategies
- have a positive attitude and a belief that problems can be solved through persistent analysis
- develop new strategies to solve particular problems when necessary
- remain open-minded during the process, maintaining a willingness to explore alternative strategies and solutions, and to accept mistakes as part of the process

New problems linked with technological change in our society are arising and our students must be able to deal with them.

Reflecting upon Knapp and Glenn's third characteristic of effective problem solvers, that they develop new strategies to solve particular problems when necessary, I couldn't help but think of my grandson, Benjamin. While eating a sandwich he began to talk with his mouth full. His grandpa told him that was bad manners and that he should not speak until his mouth was empty. After a brief pause Benjamin said, "I could push the food to one side of my mouth so that no one could see it and then I could talk, Grandpa. That wouldn't be using bad manners!" Communication, thinking, and social skills, as suggested by this example, are all interconnected with problem solving.

73

CHAPTER SEVEN

Social Skills

Great discoveries and achievements invariably
involve the co-operation of many minds.
Alexander Graham Bell

Research by W. W. Hartup suggests that peer relationships contribute greatly to both social and cognitive development. The single
best childhood predictor of how well a child will function as an
adult is not IQ, school grades, or classroom behavior, but rather,
the ease with which the child gets along with other children
(*Having Friends, Making Friends, and Keeping Friends: Relationships
as Educational Contexts*). L. G. Latz and D. McClellan suggest that
we view peer relationships as the first of the four Rs of education
(*The Teacher's Role in the Social Development of Young Children*). My
Portrait of Lifelong Learning shows social skills as an essential
transferable skill.

The best possible way to teach social skills in the classroom is
within an area of learning. For example, when Grade 4 students
studied fruits and seeds, they worked in small groups studying
the effects of pesticides on the growth of plants. Their first task
was to brainstorm what they knew and didn't know about the
effects of pesticides. Throughout this process students had multiple opportunities for practising their information and social skills,
namely, sharing, working together, cooperating, contributing
ideas, reaching agreement, taking turns, staying with the group,
and accepting responsibility. Working in a real problem-solving

environment enabled group members to hone their academic and social skills.

Exploring Social Skills

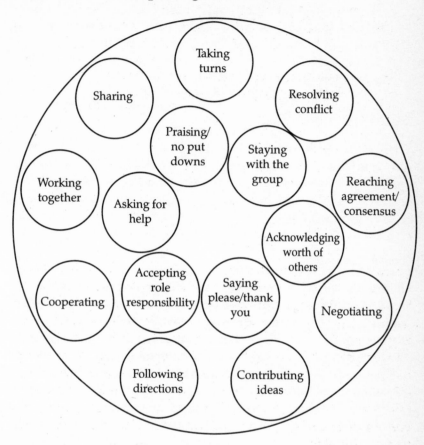

Moving Towards Cooperation

The circle graphic entitled "Exploring Social Skills" identifies some common social skills, many of which relate to cooperation. Beyond the discussion in this chapter, you might want to turn to some of the many excellent reference books that focus on social skills. These include the following:

- *Cooperative Learning: Where Heart Meets Mind*, by Barrie Bennett, Carol Rolheiser-Bennett, and Laurie Stevahn (Ajax, ON: Educational Connections, 1991)

- *Blueprints for Thinking in the Cooperative Classroom*, by James Bellanca and Robin Fogarty (Arlington Heights, IL: Skylight, 1991)
- *Structuring the Classroom Successfully for Cooperative Team Learning*, by Teresa Cantlon (Portland, OR: Prestige, 1989)
- *Together We Learn*, by Judy Clarke, Ron Wideman, and Susan Eadie (Scarborough, ON: Prentice-Hall, 1990)
- *Our Cooperative Classroom*, by David Johnson et al. (Edina, MN: Interaction Book Co., 1988)

Building Social Skills

We need to teach social skills and integrate them into the curriculum at all grade levels. Through practice these skills will become part of the students' preparation for working and living in the world. A wide variety of experiences permit the development of skills in group process.

Promoting social skills through children's literature

Children's literature is an excellent way to introduce or reinforce social skills. Its use can provide opportunities for students to learn about trust, leadership, decision making, negotiation, conflict management, and so on. Relating children's fiction to social skills allows teachers to construct a variety of experiences conducive to the development of lifelong social skills. Activities generated from the content of children's fiction can engage children in learning experiences they find enjoyable and meaningful.

You might work with children's literature in this way: (1) Choose a social skill that you would like to help develop based on the needs of your students; (2) Select a story that focuses on that skill; (3) Read the story aloud to a small group or to the whole class; (4) Use the story as a springboard into discussions on the social skill. Discuss why this skill is important to use throughout a lifetime; (5) Extend students' understanding of the skill by cooperatively developing a T-chart such as the one on page 77; (6) Follow up by asking students to generate ideas for whole-class, small-group, and individual activities to demonstrate their learning.

What is wonderful about using stories to develop social skills is that each story taps into more than one social skill. For example, *Zinnia and Dot* by Lisa Campbell Ernst taps into at least eight skills. In the story, two cranky hens, Zinnia and Dot, argue over whose eggs are more beautiful and more nearly perfect. But when a crafty weasel steals eggs, only one prize specimen is left behind. Whose is it? Will Zinnia and Dot learn to cooperate before the weasel returns? This story introduces skills ranging from resolving conflict to contributing ideas, and from following directions to working together.

I focused on the skill of working together because some of my students had difficulty doing this. We agreed this skill needed some work if we were to have a cohesive class. After I read *Zinnia and Dot* aloud and we discussed how the hens worked together, I asked the students to select a passage from the text that would illustrate the hens doing this.

> The hens, giddy from their victory, cackled as they sat back down in their nest. "One hen could never have done it," declared Dot. For once Zinnia agreed. "Lucky we both were here," she said.

We then talked about how working together is a lifelong learning skill and listed real-life situations where we would expect to demonstrate this skill. We also brainstormed for ideas on what working together looks like and sounds like, developing a Social Skills T-Chart like the one below to post in the classroom. We used it for criteria by which to measure our successes in using this skill throughout the year.

Social Skills T-Chart: Working Together

Looks like	Sounds like
Students are generating ideas.	Perhaps this would work . . .
Everyone is participating.	Agreed? Then let's do it!
Students are taking turns.	What do you think about that?
Everyone is valued.	Great job!
Everyone is on task.	I like your new approach to
Individual differences are	things.
honored.	I'm not sure if I agree.

Using *Zinnia and Dot* as the catalysts, students explored other ways to reinforce the skill. For example, they developed new stories that focused on demonstrating this skill. Students worked in groups to create their stories and took turns dramatizing the skill in the context of those stories.

The following titles are among many that promote social skills:

- *Franklin Is Bossy*, by Paulette Bourgeois
  While playing with his friends, Franklin the turtle orders them about and makes decisions on their behalf. What does he come to realize?
- *Lazy Lion*, by Mwenye Hadithi and Adrienne Kennaway
  Lion orders the other animals to build him a house on the African plain. They do their best, but Lion is proud and very difficult to please. How does he learn his lesson?
- *Tricky Tortoise*, by Mwenye Hadithi and Adrienne Kennaway
  Tortoise is tired of being trodden on by Elephant. When Elephant treads on him for the 332nd time, Tortoise develops a cunning plan to teach Elephant a lesson.
- *And You Can Be the Cat*, by Hazel Hutchins
  Leanna's brother Norman is forced to do what his sister tells him to. When they play together, Norman is always the cat. How will Norman deal with the problem? What social skill will Leanna learn?
- *Mrs. Toggle's Zipper*, by Robin Pulver
  When Mrs. Toggle's zipper sticks and traps her inside her coat, everyone in the school tries to free her, but with little success. Will working together solve Mrs. Toggle's problem?

The chart on the next page, "Organizing Children's Literature for the Development of Social Skills," indicates the range of social skills children's books can focus on.

Encouraging cooperative learning

Cooperative learning is an instructional strategy used to achieve academic and social goals. Adopting cooperative learning strategies in the classroom should help build an effective learning environment whereby students learn with and from each other. In such an environment, small groups of students function within a structured framework to accomplish set tasks or goals. For each lesson, you might teach them a new social skill or remind them of one. Overall, they should be developing interpersonal and small-group skills.

Organizing Children's Literature for the Development of Social Skills

Children's Literature Titles	Social Skills														
	1	2	3	4	5	6	7	8	9	10	11	12	13	14	15
Franklin Is Bossy	*		*			*	*	*							
Zinnia and Dot	*	*		*	*	*	*	*	*						
Lazy Lion										*		*		*	*
Tricky Tortoise								*	*						
And You Can Be the Cat		*	*		*			*					*		
Mrs. Toggle's Zipper		*	*	*	*								*		

Codes: Each number above corresponds to one of the social skills identified below.

1. Sharing
2. Working together
3. Cooperating
4. Following directions
5. Contributing ideas
6. Negotiating
7. Reaching agreement/ consensus
8. Resolving conflict
9. Taking turns
10. Praising/no put downs
11. Staying with the group
12. Asking for help
13. Accepting role responsibility
14. Saying please/thank you
15. Acknowledging work of others

There are many techniques for arranging students into groups. I have grouped them according to their interests, by the first letters of their names, by number, by favorite foods, by lifesaver colors, and by matching puzzle pieces. For strengthening team performance, I recognize the students' learning styles, putting together students of varying abilities.

Cooperative learning relies on an understanding of five basic elements: positive interdependence; individual accountability;

face-to-face interaction; social skills; and processing. In cooperative settings, every person's role is important and valued. Individuality is respected and concern for the needs of others fostered. The challenge shifts from striving to be number one to working towards a mutual goal. Everyone shares in decision making and knows it. The chart "The Cooperative Learning Environment," shows what characterizes the classroom environment when cooperative learning strategies are used effectively for group work.

The Cooperative Learning Environment	
Basic element	Looks like
Positive interdependence	There is evidence of a mutual group goal or joint group product. Materials, resources, and information are equally distributed.
Individual accountability	Individuals assume responsibility for the learning and understanding of the whole group.
Face-to-face interaction	Students work in close proximity to each other so that they can learn from each other.
Social skills	Group members communicate, listen, share, and make decisions together.
Processing	Group members reflect upon their learning to make improvements.

Within a cooperative learning environment, students talk among themselves, discuss problems, delegate tasks, and make their own decisions. Having to talk through and explain material promotes higher level reasoning strategies, as well as social skills.

Solving puzzles and games together

Stimulating hands-on resources encourage group interaction and thereby the development of social skills. In particular, you might want to use cooperative games where no one person wins or loses — everyone helps each other according to ability. Such games focus on the process, not the result. Participants have an opportunity to experience sharing and caring behavior.

My belief in the value of using cooperative games to develop social skills came from observing students arguing over marbles in the schoolyard. To foster cooperative play instead, I designed marble floor games for up to six players for indoor and outdoor use. Each board consisted of a piece of plywood one metre square with a moulding glued around the upper edge to prevent the marbles from rolling off. I elevated the board four centimetres off the floor and cut a hole in the board, inserting a cup for the marbles. The students enjoyed playing the game and requested that marble clubs be set up. As a staff, we introduced a schoolwide social skills program, Marbles, Mediation and Conflict Resolution. Many marble clubs evolved, and through teaching and reinforcing various social skills, students learned to play together in harmony.

Cooperative games such as Family Pastimes's Investigators, Sky Travelers, and Eyes of the Jungle encourage students in the Junior division to talk over decisions, share ideas, and plan strategies together. The most popular cooperative learning games include Secret Door, Princess, Harvest Time, Mountaineering, and Granny's House. Mountaineering is typical of games for children ages seven to twelve. Players form a team to try to reach the summit. They either all make it to the top — or they don't. They have to find ways to work with the elements rather than view the mountain as a sort of enemy.

Puzzles, such as Triazzle Jigsaw by Dan Gilbert, also encourage working together. The process of putting the puzzle pieces together to complete an image provides opportunities for students to practise their social skills.

Providing group experiences

Experiences, such as the Colorado project outlined in Chapter 8, allow for the practice of a wide variety of group process skills. These experiences may occur in school or in the community.

Social Skills in a Lifelong Learning Context

The development of social skills is embedded in all other parts of my Portrait of Lifelong Learning. Through interaction with their social group and participation with its members, students can strengthen personal traits. They have numerous opportunities to use their initiative, accept responsibility for their decisions, demonstrate perseverance and more while interacting with group members. As well, they can enhance verbal and written communication skills through formal and informal group discussions. Developing social skills in a group problem-solving environment lets students think through ideas and assimilate new experiences, integrating them with their own. Also, group work provides many opportunities for students to report and evaluate.

The research in favor of cooperative group learning is compelling, yet some people question how fair evaluation is and how well a teacher can ensure that students work together well. Establishing learning objectives and criteria for evaluation before students begin a learning task helps. Employing ongoing anecdotal evaluations to spot nonparticipation can also help us think more positively about cooperative group learning. Overall, the attitudes and skills that students derive from such activities are more than likely to carry over to interpersonal relationships in other settings.

Lifelong Learning Journey

We should all be concerned about the future because
we will have to spend the rest of our lives there.
                              Charles Kettering, in *Seed for Thought*

We know that the Lifelong Learning Portrait encompasses certain
principles, personal traits, and essential transferable skills, but
what does it look like when all of these components are actively
interrelated, reflecting the lifelong learner?

A Model

In August of 1996 I witnessed first hand what my Portrait of
Lifelong Learning could look like when all of the components are
fully integrated into a life experience. In Beaver Creek, Colorado,
I noticed many children gathering around a large barricaded area.
Investigating further I realized that they were at the construction
site of a community centre. Large windows cut into the boards
allowed children as well as adults to peer in and watch the workers
at work. Opportunities to look at the methods, materials, tools,
and machinery used in constructing a building abounded. As they
watched the erection of the new building, children thought of
many questions that would serve as a springboard for learning.

What made the site unique was a series of large individual
wooden boxes — individual learning centres with interactive
activities to challenge even the youngest mind — fixed to the

outside boards. The activities began with key information that was relevant to the construction site and specific to the learning activity. Questions that related to the site followed. I observed children and adults alike thinking and learning by doing and discussing.

Here is one activity from the site to engage adults and children in problem solving.

Activity on the Lighter Side
Pulleys have been used to lift heavy loads for thousands of years. The great ancient mathematician Archimedes used a compound pulley to drag a ship across a beach by himself. A pulley is a machine in which a rope passes back and forth over one or more grooved wheels. The pulley is used to make heavy loads easier to lift. Pulleys are common on most construction sites.

Challenge
How strong are you? Try pulling each of the ropes in this display.

Inquiry
Is the load lighter or heavier when multiple pulleys are used?

Relevant Learning
Look through one of the windows on the wall. Can you see any machines that are using pulleys right now?

Learners felt challenged to make connections between what they observed at the site and how their observations could be put into practice. For example, in the pulley activity children followed task card directions and manipulated materials to find out about how pulleys worked. A teacher could later refocus students' attention on the machines that used pulleys at the excavation site.

The following chart provides a model of how the components of the Lifelong Learning Portrait are interrelated and how they might be applied to the Colorado experience to reflect the lifelong learner.

Lifelong Learning and the Colorado Experience

Lifelong Learning Portrait	Colorado Experience
Principles:	
Constant change	New insights daily
Learning for everyone	Workers, community people, teachers, students
Active learning	Use of dialogue, hands-on materials
Continuous and relevant learning	Developing activity centres related to the community event
Real applications	Applications of the pulley concept to other working models
How and what of learning	Investigating and experimenting to test ideas
Learning influenced by technology	Manipulating materials, e.g., pulleys
Process of becoming	Ongoing experiences
Taking responsibility	For example: To learn the pulley concept
Nurturing inquiry	Taking a field trip — noticing things in detail, comparing, contrasting new things, asking questions, wondering if a pulley makes lifting easier
Information literacy	Thoughts develop from interaction with people, objects, events
Personal Traits:	
Curiosity	Taking a questioning approach: Is the load lighter or heavier when multiple pulleys are used?

Lifelong Learning and the Colorado Experience continued

Imagination	Follow-up: Students could make a pulley using materials from the classroom.
Initiative	Applying new knowledge of pulley concept independently
Flexibility	Taking turns at the hands-on activity centres
Risktaking	Trying out new things
Responsibility	Learning in a self-directed way
Perseverance	Staying with the problem

Essential Transferable Skills:

Communication skills	Expressing ideas accurately, coherently, and thoughtfully using oral and written language
Critical and creative thinking skills	Observing and recording, comparing and interpreting data, imagining and creating
Problem-solving skills	Finding solutions to the challenges
Social skills	Taking turns, asking for help, contributing ideas

Reflections

An experience similar to that of the Colorado field trip could happen in your own community. Field trips, whether they be to museums, art galleries, sports arenas or readily accessible neighborhood sites, can provide many benefits. They can generate group discussions, enable students to build vocabulary through concrete experiences, and encourage them to become more aware of their surroundings while sharpening their observation skills. Tapping into field trips is one way in which to bring the components of my Portrait of Lifelong Learning to life.

Lifelong Learning in a Technological Environment

Just as the seasons follow each other in an endless rhythmic cycle, so to our lifelong journey in a technological environment allows for renewal and growth. The way any of us fits my Portrait of Lifelong Learning is a snapshot at one point in time. Where we are on our lifelong learning journey is determined by our life experiences.

No one knows what new technology will alter the lives of our students, as well as of our children and grandchildren. Information technology is creating radically new jobs which students must be prepared for. We must ask ourselves how well we are preparing ourselves and our students for the technology of the future. We also need to acknowledge change and improve our school environment for learning. Let's not let today's students lose their future.

What and how students learn remain more important than the technology used to learn (noted by Jennifer Lewington in "What Are Schools Wired To?," *Globe & Mail*, June 26, 1997). Lifelong learning encompasses far more than technology. Alan November, in "Beyond Technology: Looking at the Big Picture," writes: "The real technology revolution is not about computers just as the industrial revolution was not about the steam engine. We need to look beyond the technology to seek ways of helping children become independent, critical managers of their own work" (*Elementary Curriculum*).

We must use the thinking tools that will allow us to understand the technological world around us: communication and higher level problem-solving skills, as well as scientific and technological literacy, are key. The fundamental goal is to develop students' capabilities for problem solving and critical thinking in all areas of learning.

Internalizing my Portrait of Lifelong Learning will help us achieve just that!

Nonfiction for Adults

Asselin, Marlene, Nadine Shapiro, and Jon Shapiro. *Storyworlds: Linking Minds and Imagination through Literature.* Portsmouth, NH: Heinemann, 1992.

Bellanca, James, and Robin Fogarty. *Blueprints for Thinking in the Cooperative Classroom.* Arlington Heights, IL: Skylight Training, 1991.

Bennett, Barrie, Carol Rolheiser-Bennett, and Laurie Stevahn. *Cooperative Learning: Where Heart Meets Mind.* Ajax, ON: Educational Connections, 1991.

Berthoff, Ann, ed. *Reclaiming the Imagination: Philosophical Perspectives for Writers and Teachers of Writing.* Portsmouth, NH: Boynton/Cook Publishers, 1984.

Branden, Nathaniel. *How to Raise Your Self-Esteem.* New York: Bantam, 1988.

Bransford, John D., and Barry S. Stein. *The Ideal Problem Solver.* New York: Freeman, 1995.

Cantlon, Teresa. *Structuring the Classroom Successfully for Cooperative Team Learning.* Portland, OR: Prestige, 1989.

Clarke, Judy, Ron Wideman, and Susan Eadie. *Together We Learn: Cooperative Small Group Learning.* Scarborough, ON: Prentice-Hall, 1990.

Clemmer, Jim. *Pathways to Performance: A Guide to Transforming Yourself, Your Team, and Your Organization.* Rocklin, CA: Prima, 1995.

Coloroso, Barbara. *Kids Are Worth It!* Toronto: Somerville House, 1994.

Covey, Stephen R. *The 7 Habits of Highly Effective People.* New York: Simon & Schuster Trade, 1990.

De Bono, Edward. *Six Thinking Hats.* New York: Little, Brown, 1986.

Decker, Bert. *The Art of Communicating: Achieving Interpersonal Impact in Business*. Rev. ed. Edited by Michael J. Crisp. Menlo Park, CA: Crisp Publications, 1996.

Egan, Kieran, and Dan Nadaner, ed. *Imagination and Education*. Ann Arbor, MI: Books on Demand.

Gates, Bill. *The Road Ahead*. New York: Viking Penguin, 1995.

Harlen, Wynne, ed. *Primary Science . . . Taking the Plunge: How to Teach Primary Science More Effectively*. Portsmouth, NH: Heinemann, 1985.

Hartup, W. W. *Having Friends, Making Friends, and Keeping Friends: Relationships as Educational Contexts*. Urbana, IL: ERIC Clearinghouse, 1992.

Hoff, Benjamin. *The Tao of Pooh*. New York: Viking Penguin, 1983.

ICA Staff. *Winning through Participation*. Dubuque, IA: Kendall-Hunt Publishing Co., 1989.

Johnson, David, and Frank Johnson. *Joining Together: Group Theory and Group Skills*. 5th ed. Needham Heights, MA: Allyn & Bacon, 1993.

Johnson, David, et al. *Our Cooperative Classroom*. Edina, MN: Interaction Book, 1988.

Knapp, Lynda R., and Allen D. Glenn. *Restructuring Schools with Technology*. Needham Heights, MA: Allyn & Bacon, 1996.

Kruise, Carol S. *Those Bloomin' Books: A Handbook for Extending Thinking Skills*. Englewood, CO: Libraries Unlimited, 1987.

Labinowicz, Ed. *The Piaget Primer: Thinking, Learning, Teaching*. Reading, MA: Addison-Wesley, 1980.

Latz, L. G., and D. McClellan. *The Teacher's Role in the Social Development of Young Children*. Urbana, IL: ERIC Clearinghouse, 1991.

Logan, Robert K. *The Fifth Language: Learning a Living in the Computer Age*. Toronto: Stoddart, 1995.

Mandel, Steve. *Effective Presentation Skills*. 2nd rev. ed. Edited by Philip Gerould. Menlo Park, CA: Crisp Publications, 1993.

Mandel, Steve. *Technical Presentation Skills*. Rev. ed. Edited by Philip Gerould. Menlo Park, CA: Crisp Publications, 1994.

McLuhan, Marshall. *Understanding Media: The Extensions of Man*. Cambridge, MA: MIT Press, 1994.

Miller, John. *The Holistic Curriculum*. Toronto: Ontario Institute for Studies in Education, 1988.

Morgan, Gareth. *Imaginization: The Art of Creative Management*. Newbury Park, CA: Sage Publishers, 1993.

Naisbitt, John. *Global Paradox*. New York: Morrow, 1994.

Pauker, Robert A. *Teaching Thinking and Reasoning Skills*. Edited by Ben Brodinsky. Arlington, VA: The American Association of School Administrators, 1987.

Pisek, Paul. *Creativity, Innovation and Quality*. Milwaukee, WI: ASQC Press, 1997.

Polya, Gyorgy. *How to Solve It*. Princeton, NJ: Princeton University Press, 1971.

Senge, Peter M. *The Fifth Discipline: Mastering the Five Practices of the Learning Organization*. New York: Doubleday, 1990.

Tapscott, Don, and Art Caston. *Paradigm Shift: The New Promise of Information Technology*. New York: McGraw-Hill, 1990.

Tapscott, Don. *The Digital Economy: Promise and Peril in the Age of Networked Intelligence*. New York: McGraw-Hill, 1996.

Toffler, Alvin. *Learning for Tomorrow: The Role of the Future in Education*. New York: Random House, 1974.

Toffler, Alvin. *The Third Wave*. New York: Bantam, 1984.

Toffler, Alvin. *Future Shock*. New York: Bantam, 1984.

Toffler, Alvin. *Powershift: Knowledge, Wealth, and Violence at the Edge of the 21st Century*. New York: Bantam, 1991.

Toffler, Alvin, and Heidi Toffler. *Creating a New Civilization: The Politics of the Third Wave*. Atlanta, GA: Turner Publishing, 1995.

Trelease, Jim. *Jim Trelease's Read-Aloud Handbook*. 4th ed. New York: Viking Penguin, 1995.

Udall, Anne J., and Joan E. Daniels. *Creating the Thoughtful Classroom: Strategies to Promote Student Thinking*. Tucson, AZ: Zephyr Press, 1991.

Wiederhold, Chuck. *Cooperative Learning and Higher Level Thinking: The Question Matrix*. Rev. ed. San Juan Capistrano, CA: Kagan Cooperative, 1991.

Nonfiction for Children

Anderson, Joan. *From Map to Museum: Uncovering Mysteries of the Past*. New York: Morrow, 1988.

Crockett, Tom, and Tim Gangwen, ed. *Visual Learning Guide and Activity Book*. New York: Polaroid Education Program, 1994.

Golick, Margie. *Wacky Word Games*. Markham, ON: Pembroke Publishers, 1995.

Greenwood, Barbara, and Bob Greenwood. *Speak Up! Speak Out! Every Kid's Guide to Planning, Preparing, and Presenting a Speech*. Markham, ON: Pembroke Publishers, 1995.

Heller, Ruth. *A Cache of Jewels*. New York: Putnam, 1992.

Heller, Ruth. *Kites Sail High: A Book about Verbs*. New York: Putnam, 1988.

Heller, Ruth. *Many Luscious Lollipops: A Book about Adjectives*. New York: Sandcastle Books, 1992.

Hoare, Nick, and Simon Melhuish, ed. *Mind-Bending Classic Logic Puzzles*. Kingston, U.K.: Lagoon Trading Co., 1996.

Kramer, Stephen P. *How to Think Like a Scientist*. New York: HarperCollins Children's Books, 1987.

Macaulay, David. *The Way Things Work*. Boston: Houghton Mifflin, 1988.

Needham, Kate, and Gay Gibson. *Collecting Things*. Tulsa, OK: Usborne, 1995.

Pederson, Ted, and Francis Moss. *Internet for Kids: A Beginner's Guide to Surfing the Net*. Los Angeles, CA: Price/Stern/Sloan, 1995.

Pitter, Keiko, et al. *Every Student's Guide to the Internet*. New York: McGraw-Hill, 1995.

Roalf, Peggy. *Circus*. New York: Hyperion Child, 1993.

Schepp, Debra, and Brad Schepp. *Kidnet: The Kid's Guide to Surfing through Cyberspace*. New York: HarperCollins, 1995.

Shimkofsky, Wendy Ashton. *Brainstorm!* Markham, ON: Pembroke Publishers, 1996.

Steer, Dugald. *Mythical Mazes*. Dorking, U.K.: Templar Publishing, 1996.

Stinson, Kathy. *Writing Your Best Picture Book Ever*. Markham, ON: Pembroke Publishers, 1990.

Wilson, April. *Look Again! The Second Ultimate Spot-the-Difference Book*. New York: Dial Books for Young Readers, 1992.

Children's Literature

Allen, Pamela. *Mr. Archimedes' Bath*. New York: HarperCollins World, 1991.

Andersen, Hans Christian. *The Top and the Ball*. Nashville, TN: Ideals Child, 1991.

Baker, Jeannie. *Window*. New York: Greenwillow, 1991.

Base, Graeme. *The Eleventh Hour: A Curious Mystery*. Toronto: Stoddart, 1988.

Booth, David, ed. *Til All the Stars Have Fallen*. Toronto: Kids Can Press, 1987.

Bourgeois, Paulette. *Franklin Is Bossy*. Toronto: Kids Can Press, 1993.

Browne, Anthony. *The Tunnel*. London, U.K.: Walker Books, 1993.

Browne, Anthony. *Through the Magic Mirror*. London, U.K.: Puffin Books, 1995.

Browne, Anthony. *Willy the Wimp*. Toronto: Random House of Canada, 1989.

Browne, Eileen. *No Problem*. London, U.K.: Walker Books, 1993.

Bunting, Eve. *The Wall*. Boston, MA: Houghton Mifflin, 1992.

Bunting, Eve. *The Wednesday Surprise*. New York: Clarion Books, 1990.

Carle, Eric. *Papa, Please Get the Moon for Me*. Saxonville, MA: Picture Book Studio, 1991.

Clement, Claude. *The Voice of the Wood*. Translated by Lenny Hort. New York: Dial Books, 1989.

Cole, Joanna. *The Magic School Bus Lost in the Solar System*. New York: Scholastic, 1992.

Cox, Phil Roxbee. *Whatever Happened to Professor Potts?* (Solve It Yourself Series) Tulsa, OK: Usborne, 1995.

Demi. *The Empty Pot*. Markham, ON: Fitzhenry & Whiteside, 1990.

De Paola, Tomie. *The Hunter and the Animals*. New York: Holiday House, 1981.

Dunn, Sonja. *Primary Rhymerry*. Markham, ON: Pembroke Publishers, 1993.

Dunrea, Olivier. *Deep Down Underground*. New York: Simon & Schuster Children's, 1993.

Ernst, Lisa Campbell. *Zinnia and Dot*. New York: Viking Children's Books, 1992.

Gamble, Judi, and Robert McConnell. *Gobley for Mayor!* Toronto: Napoleon Publishing, 1991.

Giganti, Jr., Paul. *How Many Snails? A Counting Book*. Edited by Amy Cohn. New York: Morrow, 1994.

Gilman, Phoebe. *Something from Nothing*. Richmond Hill, ON: Scholastic Canada, 1991.

Hadithi, Mwenye. *Lazy Lion*. London, U.K.: Hodder, 1992.

Hadithi, Mwenye. *Tricky Tortoise*. London, U.K.: Hodder, 1990.

Hutchins, Hazel. *And You Can Be the Cat*. Toronto: Annick, 1992.

Jonas, Ann. *The 13th Clue*. New York: Greenwillow, 1992.

Joyce, William. *A Day with Wilbur Robinson*. New York: HarperCollins Children's Books, 1990.

King, Christopher. *The Boy Who Ate the Moon*. New York: Philomel Books, 1988.

Kirk, David. *Miss Spider's Tea Party*. New York: Scholastic, 1984.

Lobel, Arnold. *The Rose in My Garden*. New York: Greenwillow, 1984.

MacGill-Callahan, Sheila. *And Still the Turtle Watched*. Markham, ON: Penguin, 1991.

Mahy, Margaret. *The Boy with Two Shadows*. London, U.K.: Puffin Books, 1996.

Markle, Sandra. *Science Mini-Mysteries: Easy to Do Experiments Designed to Keep You Guessing*. New York: Atheneum-Macmillan Publishing, 1988.

McPhail, David. *Andrew's Bath*. New York: Little, Brown & Co., 1984.

Micklethwait, Lucy. *I Spy: An Alphabet in Art*. New York: Morrow, 1996.

Noonan, Diana. *The Tricky Sticky Problem*. New Zealand: Learning Media, 1996.

Noonan, Diana. *Whizz! Click!* New Zealand: Learning Media, 1996.

Packard, Edward. *The Cave of Time* (Choose Your Own Adventure). New York: Bantam, 1982.

Pallotta, Jerry. *The Icky Bug Alphabet Book*. Watertown, MA: Charlesbridge, 1986.

Piper, Watty. *The Little Engine That Could*. New York: Platt & Munk, 1991.

Pulver, Robin. *Mrs. Toggle and the Dinosaur*. New York: Simon & Schuster Children's, 1995.

Pulver, Robin. *Mrs. Toggle's Zipper*. New York: Simon & Schuster Children's, 1993.

Rosenberg, Liz. *The Carousel*. San Diego, CA: Harcourt Brace, 1995.

Schneider, Elisa. *The Merry-Go-Round Dog*. Toronto: Random House of Canada, 1988.

Scieszka, Jon. *Math Curse*. New York: Viking Children's Books, 1995.

Scieszka, Jon. *The True Story of the Three Little Pigs*. New York: Viking Children's Books, 1989.

Steig, William. *Abel's Island*. New York: Farrar, Straus & Giroux, 1976.

Tabor, Roger. *Survival: Could You Be a Fox?* Toronto: Macmillan of Canada, 1989.

Thaler, Mike. *How Far Will a Rubber Band Stretch?* New York: Simon & Schuster, 1990.

Tompart, Ann. *Grandfather Tang's Story*. New York: Crown, 1990.

Trivizas, Eugene. *The Three Little Wolves and the Big Bad Pig*. New York: Macmillan Publishing, 1993.

Turnbull, Ann. *The Sand Horse*. New York: Simon & Schuster Children's, 1989.

Van Allsburg, Chris. *Just a Dream*. Boston: Houghton Mifflin, 1990.

Van Allsburg, Chris. *The Wretched Stone*. Boston: Houghton Mifflin, 1991.

Viorst, Judith. *Earrings!* New York: Simon & Schuster Children's, 1993.

Wiesner, David. *Free Fall*. New York: Morrow, 1991.

Wiesner, David. *June 29, 1999*. New York: Clarion Books, 1992.

Williams, Barbara. *Albert's Tooth*. London, U.K.: Puffin, 1974.

Williams, Margery. *The Velveteen Rabbit*. New York: Avon Books, 1982.

Wilson, Sarah. *The Day That Henry Cleaned His Room*. New York: Simon & Schuster, 1990.

Wood, Audrey. *King Bidgood's in the Bathtub*. San Diego, CA: Harcourt Brace, 1993.

Wynne-Jones, Tim. *Zoom at Sea*. Toronto: Groundwood, 1990.

Wynne-Jones, Tim. *Zoom Upstream*. Toronto: Groundwood, 1992.

Yee, Paul. *Roses Sing on New Snow*. Toronto: Groundwood, 1991.

Index

Acknowledgments

I got the idea for this book while sitting at my mother's kitchen table discussing the issues and concerns facing today's schools. Then 88 years of age, my mother reflected upon "rote learning" as the main method for delivering education in what was a farming community. What interested me most about our conversation was that she felt her learning — she had attended a one-room schoolhouse with all grades combined — had been a truly continuous endeavor. Thanks, Mom, for sharing your past experiences in education and for role-modelling the importance of lifelong learning throughout your life. I learned from the best!

Thanks to my son Jonathan, who brought to life my thoughts and ideas by using his expertise in computers to create my original graphic designs. As well, I would like to thank my husband, Maurice, for being a good listener and for challenging my ideas along the way. Without his diligent advice, I might have settled for something less.

I wish to extend thanks to Mary Jean Clark, of Many Colours in Port Perry, Ontario, for her advice on the children's literature I recommend throughout this book; also, to Wendy Schreiber, of CCT Software, for providing CD-ROMs for me to explore. Finally, I couldn't forget to mention my students; my grandson, Benjamin; and friends and colleagues who have provided a wealth of information and support as always.